"Investing is a continuous process of learning, and it will be a rare investor who does not glean substantive lessons from the notable AKO story of quality investing."

– Stephen Blyth, President and CEO, Harvard Management Company, Professor of the Practice of Statistics, Harvard University

"Capturing both the science and the art that have driven AKO's success, *Quality Investing* is equal parts investing handbook and ode to the beauty of truly great businesses."

– Peter H. Ammon, Chief Investment Officer, University of Pennsylvania

"*Quality Investing* answers the riddle of what you get when you cross Peter Lynch's One Up on Wall Street with Seth Klarman's Margin of Safety. By combining a discerning eye for sustainable growth with a disciplined calculus to buy over horizons when the probabilities are favorable, the book articulates a profitable approach to the art of investing."

– Jason Klein, Senior Vice President & Chief Investment Officer, Memorial Sloan Kettering Cancer Center

"I recommend *Quality Investing* highly as a guide to harness the power of core investment principles. Shows why the best long-term 'margin of safety' comes not from an investment's price but from the value of a company's competitive advantage."

– Thomas A. Russo, Partner, Gardner, Russo & Gardner

"*Quality Investing*, from a team of top quality investors, provides a clear and rigorous analysis of a highly successful, long-term investment strategy. In an increasingly short-term investment world, the book's insights are likely to remain hugely valuable."

– Neil Ostrer, Founder, Marathon Asset Management

"*Quality Investing* describes a unique approach to evaluating investment opportunities based on real life examples and experience. Replete with interesting lessons and insights relevant not just for investors, but for any business leader seeking to build an enduring, high-quality company, *Quality Investing* is an outstanding book and should be required reading for business leaders and MBA students as well as for investors."

– Henrik Ehrnrooth, President & CEO, KONE

"The book is a crisply-written mix of sound investment principles, insightful commercial patterns, and colorful business cases. A real pleasure to read."

– Hassan Elmasry, Founder and Lead Portfolio Manager, Independent Franchise Partners

"AKO Capital were one of the first to recognise Ryanair's secret formula... An outstandingly handsome CEO, a brilliant strategy, all underpinned with our innate humility. These guys are geniuses. For a better life you must read this book... and fly Ryanair!!"

– Michael O'Leary, Chief Executive, Ryanair

"Quality counts. If you are a long term investor, it's hard to find a more important factor as to what will power your ultimate investment returns. That said, quality is impossible to measure with precision because it often embodies more subjective qualitative factors than easily quantifiable measurements. Quality is also dynamic and changes over time. This book attempts through case studies, descriptions, and quantifiable measurement to help investors think systematically about quality and its importance. Enjoy!"

– Thomas S. Gayner, President and Chief Investment Officer, Markel Corporation

"An indispensable addition to any value investing library, *Quality Investing* will appeal to novices and experts alike. Vivid real-life case studies make for an engaging read that shows the power of compounding that comes with owning high-quality businesses for the long term."

– John Mihaljevic, 'The Manual of Ideas'

"An excellent read: clear and insightful. *Quality Investing* is an important aid to shareholders when evaluating any company."

– Albert Baehny, Chairman, Geberit

"*Quality Investing* is an outstanding resource for all investors seeking to enhance their knowledge of the critical drivers for investment success. Several important concepts for discerning and evaluating outstanding companies are clearly explained and further elaborated upon through many specific company examples. I highly recommend *Quality Investing* to all prospective investors from beginners to experienced practitioners."

– Paul Lountzis, Lountzis Asset Management, LLC

Quality Investing

Quality Investing

Owning the best companies for the
long term

**Lawrence A. Cunningham, Torkell T. Eide
and Patrick Hargreaves**

HARRIMAN HOUSE LTD
18 College Street
Petersfield
Hampshire
GU31 4AD
GREAT BRITAIN
Tel: +44 (0)1730 233870
Email: enquiries@harriman-house.com
Website: www.harriman-house.com

First published in Great Britain in 2016
Copyright © AKO Capital LLP

The right of Lawrence A. Cunningham, Torkell T. Eide and Patrick Hargreaves to be identified as the authors has been asserted in accordance with the Copyright, Design and Patents Act 1988.

Print ISBN: 978-0-85719-501-2
eBook ISBN: 978-0-85719-512-8

British Library Cataloguing in Publication Data
A CIP catalogue record for this book can be obtained from the British Library.

Printed and bound by CPI Group (UK) Ltd, Croydon, CR0 4YY

CONTENTS

Case studies

About the authors

Lawrence A. Cunningham has written a dozen books, including *The Essays of Warren Buffett: Lessons for Corporate America*, published in successive editions since 1996 in collaboration with the legendary Mr. Buffett; the critically acclaimed *Berkshire Beyond Buffett: The Enduring Value of Values* (Columbia University Press 2014); and *Contracts in the Real World: Stories of Popular Contracts and Why They Matter* (Cambridge University Press 2012). Cunningham's op-eds have been published in many newspapers worldwide, including the *Financial Times*, *New York Times*, and *Wall Street Journal*, and his research has appeared in top academic journals published by such universities as Columbia, Harvard, and Vanderbilt. A popular professor at George Washington University, Cunningham also lectures widely, delivering as many as 50 lectures annually to a wide variety of academic, business and investing groups.

Torkell Tveitevoll Eide is a Portfolio Manager at AKO Capital. He rejoined AKO in 2013 from SKAGEN Funds in Norway where he spent four years as a Portfolio Manager on SKAGEN's $9 billion global equity fund. Prior to that Eide had spent three years at AKO Capital as an investment analyst, and before AKO he was a Management Consultant with McKinsey & Company in its

Corporate Finance practice. Eide has a first-class degree in Economics from the London School of Economics and Political Science.

Patrick Hargreaves is a Portfolio Manager at AKO Capital. Before joining AKO in 2011, he spent eight years at Goldman Sachs where he ran the European Small & MidCap Research team before becoming Deputy Head of the Pan-European research department. Prior roles include stints at Cazenove and PricewaterhouseCoopers, where he qualified as a Chartered Accountant. Hargreaves has a degree in English Literature from Oxford University.

Acknowledgments

We would all like to thank Richard Pearce, who was instrumental in every phase of the book's evolution (and who somehow retained his sense of humor throughout the process).

Cunningham would also like to thank Stephanie Cuba, editorial maven extraordinaire, and Lillian White, for administrative assistance.

Eide and Hargreaves would also like to thank Myles Hunt, Craig Pearce and Suzanne Tull at Harriman House, Alice Waugh for her sagacious advice and scrupulous copy-editing, and their colleagues at AKO Capital for invaluable input. In particular, they would single out Gorm Thomassen for his wise counsel and Nicolai Tangen for his support, guidance and inspirational leadership. Were it not for their vision and insatiable desire to learn from mistakes, this book would not have been possible. Sincere thanks.

*"Quality is never an accident;
it is always the result of intelligent effort."*

John Ruskin

PREFACE

THIS BOOK BEGAN AS A SMALL INTERNAL project at AKO Capital, an equity fund based in London that has enjoyed a compound annual growth rate more than double that of the market (9.4% per annum versus the MSCI Europe's 3.9%)[1] and delivered excess returns of approximately 8% per annum on its long book[2] since inception a decade ago. The project's initial scope was to institutionalize lessons learned from refining the fund's quality-focused investment philosophy over that time. What we have come to understand is that successful investing involves a degree of pattern recognition: while industries and companies are diverse and economic environments endlessly changing, strongly performing investments tend to have commonalities. Making sense of these commonalities can help build a strong investment portfolio.

After amassing a substantial body of material to share with new members of the AKO team – and to remind veterans of what they had once learned but might by now have forgotten – it became obvious that the results should be shared with the fund's investors as well. Clients have the right to know as much as practically possible about the stewardship of their funds. After all, a strong long-term partnership, in business as well as in private life, works best when based on trust and openness.

As the project expanded, AKO recruited Lawrence A. Cunningham, the noted American author of investing and business books, to join us. As we refined and honed the material together, it appeared suitable for a yet wider audience of investors and business analysts, as well as managers. The result is the book you are reading, which offers an account of quality investing along with numerous case studies to illustrate the attributes of quality companies.

We do not posit that a quality-based strategy is the only route to investment success. But we maintain that taking time to understand the fundamental attributes of a company – from its industry position to its sources of long-term growth – is relevant for all investors, regardless of style. The concept of this book is to distill a considerable body of practical knowledge developed through long-term ownership of some great companies – as well as a few that flattered to deceive.

While the genesis of the book lay in identifying the patterns evident in quality companies, we have supplemented this with additional material to provide context. This includes explaining what quality is from both a financial and an operational perspective, examining the characteristics that help to foster quality, and finally outlining the challenges and some potential mistake-reduction strategies.

There are quality companies everywhere, from America to Asia. The examples given in this book are primarily of European companies, largely due to AKO Capital's deeper heritage in the European equities market. We believe that lessons from one continent can be applied on a global scale and are therefore relevant to all investors as well as to managers and business analysts.

A cynic might say that writing a book about investing is playing odds that prudent investors would normally disfavor in financial markets: only a small number of investment books stand the test of time or even remain worthwhile reads for long. Examples of great companies can suddenly seem outdated or just plain wrong, and observations that appeared insightful when written can end up looking foolish.

We appreciate that some of the assertions made in this book will almost certainly be disproved or become obsolete. As with most important and interesting things in life, investing is a continuous learning exercise and all any book can do is reflect the knowledge or beliefs prevailing at the time of writing. While we are confident that the fundamental principle of long-term ownership of quality companies is a sensible one, new lessons and patterns will keep emerging. We, like other investors, will continue to adapt to them.

London and New York
October 2015

INTRODUCTION

THE CONCEPT OF QUALITY IS FAMILIAR. PEOPLE make judgments about it every day. Yet articulating a clear definition of quality is challenging. Open most dictionaries and you will see a dozen or more sub-definitions for the word; none of which, incidentally, makes any reference to quality in a corporate or investing context. Despite the shadowy semantics, it is still a powerful word. Everyone has strong opinions on quality. One of our favorite explanations appears in *Zen and the Art of Motorcycle Maintenance*, in which Phaedrus tells his students that "… even though Quality cannot be defined, you know what Quality is!"[3]

By comparison, value investing is relatively simple and well-understood (if tough to execute). Ask professional investors what they take value investing to mean, and responses will likely be consistent; but ask the same people what they think quality investing means, and responses will vary widely. Core answers might coalesce around some key themes, such as strong management and attractive growth. But beyond these central elements, interpretations tend to diverge. This is because in investing as well as in other fields, 'quality' resists a tidy definition, involving as it does an overlapping matrix of traits and, ultimately, judgment.

The best companies often appear to be characterized by an ineffable something, much like that of people who seem graced by a lucky gene. Think about those of your peers who seem a lot like you but somehow always catch a break. They are not obviously smarter, smoother, richer, or better-looking than you, yet they are admitted to their university of choice, get their dream job, and earn considerable wealth. Try to discern what they have that you don't, and you are stumped. Chalk it up to fate or plain dumb luck.

Businesses can be similar. For reasons that are not always evident, some end up doing the right things with better results than average. They may not appear to be savvier acquirers, more adept marketers, or bolder pioneers, yet they integrate new businesses better, launch products more successfully, and open new markets with fewer mishaps. Perhaps through some combination of vision, scale, or business philosophy, these companies uncannily come out ahead. They seem to be governed by Yhprum's Law, so that if anything can go right, it will. But it is unlikely that such corporate success is the result of mere providence. Quality investing is a way to pinpoint the specific traits, aptitudes and patterns that increase the probability of a particular company prospering over time – as well as those that decrease such chances.

In our view, three characteristics indicate quality. These are strong, predictable cash generation; sustainably high returns on capital; and attractive growth opportunities. Each of these financial traits is attractive in its own right, but combined, they are particularly powerful, enabling a virtuous circle of cash generation, which can be reinvested at high rates of return, begetting more cash, which can be reinvested again.

A simple example illustrates their power. Say a company generates free cash flow of $100 million annually. Its return on invested capital is 20% and it has ample opportunity to reinvest all cash in expansion at the same rate. Sustained for ten years, this cycle of cash generation and reinvestment would drive a greater than six-fold increase in free cash. Albert Einstein famously referred to compound interest as the eighth wonder of the world. Compound growth in cash flow can be equally miraculous.

The profound point is that the critical link between growth and value creation is the return on incremental capital. Since share prices tend to follow earnings over the long term, the more capital that can be deployed at high rates of return to drive greater earnings growth, the more valuable a company becomes. Warren Buffett summarized the point best: "Leaving the question of price aside, the best business to own is one that over an extended period can employ large amounts of incremental capital at very high rates of return."[4] The best investments, in other words, combine strong growth with high returns on capital.

It is relatively easy to identify a company that generates high returns on capital or which has delivered strong historical growth – there are plenty of screening tools which make this possible. The more challenging analytical endeavor is assessing the characteristics that combine to enable and sustain these appealing financial outputs.

Above all, the structure of a company's industry is critical to its potential as a quality investment: even the best-run company in an over-supplied, price-deflationary industry is unlikely to warrant consideration. On top of this, there are bottom-up, company-specific factors that must be understood. In combination with attractive industry structures, these form the building blocks which can enable a company to deliver sustained operational outperformance and attractive long-term earnings growth.

The characteristics we describe in this book are appealing whether an investor owns the entire business or fractional shares in it. Indeed, there are many similarities between owning shares in a listed company and being the private owner of the same business. The value any business creates, listed or not, is determined by the rate at which it deploys incremental capital. And the predictability of cash flow and growth is equally important, analytically identical, and with the same risk, whether a company has a daily price quote or not.

The key difference facing equity investors is that they must find companies in the stock market, where theory suggests that the superior attributes of quality companies would be fairly reflected in price, offering no investing advantage. But while premiums are paid for shares of such businesses, they are frequently insufficient.

Valuation premiums of quality companies often reflect some degree of *expected* operational outperformance, but actual performance tends to exceed expectations over time. Stock prices thus tend to undervalue quality companies.[5]

Chapter One identifies the features that exhibit the potential for a quality investment. It begins by tracing a line from a process of effective capital deployment through the achievement of sustainably high return on that capital to superior earnings growth. In this chapter we also explore the building blocks that can help companies deliver attractive financial outputs. These include an appealing industry structure, multiple sources of prospective growth, high-value customer benefits, various forms of competitive advantage, and good management.

Quality investing requires an understanding of how a company achieves its attractive economic characteristics to ensure that they are sustainable. Chapter Two, the analytical heart of the book, distills our collective experience into a dozen patterns that enable quality companies in different industries to deliver strong financial results. These range from the more obvious (lowest unit-cost producers) to the more esoteric (friendly middlemen), and unite an otherwise diverse group of businesses in different industries from agriculture to plumbing and banking. The patterns are direct routes to generating strong, predictable and sustainable cash flows, growth, and returns on capital.

Such attractive economic characteristics may also arise from factors more transient or vulnerable to disruption, which may detract from a company's quality. Chapter Three explores prominent examples of such potential pitfalls, such as an economic franchise that depends on government discretion or product offerings that are susceptible to obsolescence amid shifting consumer preferences. In this chapter we lead with a discussion of cyclicality. Upturns can make companies look stronger than they are, yet can also be exploited advantageously by some quality companies.

Chapter Four turns to the implementation of a quality investing strategy, outlining the challenges and the areas where mistakes recur. Challenges include combating prevailing propensities to respond to short-term shifts and coping with the tendency to place greater weight on numerical analysis than on qualitative analysis. Mistakes include letting macroeconomic indicators influence what should be bottom-up business analysis. We explain why quality investing stresses qualitative characteristics more than quantitative valuation, and some techniques we have found useful in reducing mistakes in the process.

The book includes more than 20 case studies, most of them of quality companies and the attributes and patterns that give them the edge, but we also provide examples of mistakes – companies that we bought thinking they were quality businesses but about which we were proved to be incorrect. Among well-known global titans that epitomize attractive traits we feature Diageo, Hermès, L'Oréal, and Unilever; among powerhouses without such universal name recognition we present global leaders in the manufacture and service of elevators, locks, and plumbing fixtures; makers of chemicals used in agriculture, medicine, and yogurt; a discount airline and apparel retailer; two eyewear makers and distributors; a credit information behemoth; and even a bank. On the downside we feature two household names – Nokia and Tesco – along with a dental implant maker, a medical equipment manufacturer and an oilfield services provider.

This book is a reflection of our journey through the years in quality investing. We have learned a lot along the way and are glad to be able to share our experiences with you.

CHAPTER ONE
BUILDING BLOCKS

FOR THE PAST 20 YEARS, ORGANIC SALES GROWTH at French cosmetics giant L'Oréal has been phenomenally consistent, averaging over 6% with only one year of contraction, in 2009. The company has maintained a strong post-tax return on capital, which has gradually increased from the mid to high teens over the same period. Its cash conversion track-record has also been consistently strong.

Although L'Oréal's organic growth rates would not qualify it as a 'growth' stock, this combination of traits has driven extraordinary long-term results. L'Oréal's earnings growth has compounded by 11% over this 20-year period, and the stock price has increased over 1,000%, outperforming the broader market nearly five-fold in the process.

Stellar shareholder returns largely reflect the virtuous circle of L'Oréal's sustained cash generation and effective cash deployment. The company has invested heavily in both research and development (R&D) as well as marketing and promotion, and has acquired a number of new brands, the returns on which have been attractive. Excess capital has been diverted into paying a steadily increasing dividend and reducing its shares outstanding by more than 10% through buybacks.

L'Oréal exemplifies the benefits that can accrue from the combination of a supportive industry structure, a management team willing to invest in growth, a differentiated product offering and a unique set of competitive advantages. These factors are what have enabled the company to deliver long-term financial success and to take advantage of its attractive set of growth opportunities. In other words, these are the building blocks of a quality company. They are crucial to the delivery and sustainability of the attractive financial traits we seek.

This chapter discusses each of these important financial and non-financial building blocks in turn. We start with a discussion of return on capital and growth, before looking at how management teams can affect a company's prospects. Finally, we delve into the ways different industry structures, customer benefits and competitive advantages can affect an assessment of quality.

A. CAPITAL ALLOCATION

A company can choose to allocate capital in one of four main ways: capital expenditures for growth; advertising and promotion or R&D; mergers and acquisitions; or distributions to shareholders through dividends or share buybacks. We review each of these in turn, as well as briefly considering working capital, an underappreciated aspect of capital deployment. These capital allocation decisions are some of the most critical a company makes, and are the difference between creating value and destroying it.

GROWTH CAPEX

Companies typically refer to all internal investments as capital expenditures, but there is an important distinction between capital expenditures required for maintenance and those incurred for growth or expansion. Unlike growth capital expenditures, maintenance capital expenditures are required just to maintain the status quo. This form of capital outlay is therefore equivalent to ordinary operating expenses and should be relatively predictable. Growth capex, as the term suggests, is the deployment of capital for the purposes of generating organic growth. Examples might include the construction of a new plant to increase production capacity, or investment in new stores for a leisure or retail concept.

Today, Swedish fashion retailer H&M operates from more than 3,500 stores globally, up from less than 1,200 in 2005. In 2014, the company opened the equivalent of more than one outlet every day. Despite relatively modest like-for-like sales growth (averaging a shade above 1% for the last ten years), H&M's solid returns on its new store investment, even adjusted for leases, have enabled the group to more than double per-share earnings over this period.

Such performance in capital allocation is laudable. Sustaining high returns on incremental organic capex in this way yields significant compound growth, making it our preferred use of capital where the right investment opportunities exist.

INVESTMENT IN R&D AND ADVERTISING AND PROMOTION (A&P)

Today's impressive sales of Dove soap, made by Unilever, result largely from decades of historical marketing spending to build the brand. By creating brand awareness, Unilever invested, in effect, in the consumer's consciousness. It bought a mental barrier to entry, as rivals would need to spend substantial sums to replace the brand in the minds of consumers. While ongoing brand advertising is needed to sustain awareness – an outlay best seen as equivalent to maintenance capital expenditures – a large portion is aimed at influencing new generations of consumers. This is more comparable to growth capex.

In many industries, spending on advertising is an important launch pad for a company's competitive advantage and future growth. While some advertising efforts drive current sales, such as in-store exhibits, the real value accrues from sustained campaigns aimed at brand building. Unlike constructing factories or buying equipment, brand spending creates no tangible asset that can be appraised and depreciated. From a financial viewpoint, it is money out the door just as much as rent and rates. Unlike many other cost items, however, it can create lasting value.

So while financial statements classify advertising costs as expenses, they are often better conceived of as investments. This reclassification makes sense because advertising is also a far more flexible expenditure than most costs. Amid challenging economic times, advertising can be scaled back relatively quickly, adding agility to protect and manage cash flows. However, paring back too far, or for too long, can lead to long-term value erosion.

R&D costs are similar to advertising. While contemporary accounting rules allow companies to treat some R&D disbursements more like long-term assets, we focus explicitly on their dual nature: some are properly seen as expenses necessary to maintain a business, while others, the vastly larger proportion, are best viewed as investments in future growth.

Measuring returns on R&D and advertising outlay can be challenging. For R&D, in particular, there are many industries where a return will not be recovered for many years. Appropriately capitalizing these expenses is a start, but a company's long-term track record of generating returns on its R&D outlay is often the best indicator of R&D efficiency.

MERGERS AND ACQUISITIONS

Acquisitions are a common source of value destruction, so it is usually better for capital to be deployed on organic growth as opposed to M&A. That said, there are a few contexts in which acquisitions can create value for shareholders. Consolidation of fragmented industries is often an appealing rationale for growth through acquisitions. Such roll-ups, as they are often called, do not invariably succeed,[6] but there are several notable examples of successes.

For example, Essilor, a global leader in making lenses for eyeglasses, has a long history of small bolt-on acquisitions. Individually insignificant, these have become material in aggregate, adding more than 3% in annual sales per year for the last decade. These purchases are most commonly of local optical labs that give Essilor access to a local customer base and better control of its value chain. Pre-acquisition, Essilor might represent 40% of a lab's lens sales, whereas after closing, it would double that level. Given the specialized niche and deal size, there is scant competition in this acquisition market, enabling Essilor to purchase companies on attractive terms (such as six to seven times cash flow). This ability to systematically improve the operations of acquired businesses is rare but can create significant value.

Another strategy that can yield good outcomes is buying a business that is already strong. A paradigm occurred in 2007 in the eyewear market, when Luxottica, an established business offering a variety of products including sports eyewear, acquired Oakley, an already successful brand entirely focused on sports eyewear. While operations remain largely autonomous, Luxottica multiplied Oakley's distribution channels and created crossover branding to other premium fashion products, including women's wear.

We estimate that Oakley's sales growth has increased by 10% per annum under Luxottica's ownership, double the market rate during the period, and that margins have meaningfully increased. During this time, Oakley has cemented its position as an iconic sunglass brand, expanded its optical presence, and helped to enhance Luxottica's dominance in the premium eyewear industry. While we are generally skeptical of mergers rationalized on the basis of over-optimistic and loosely defined synergies,[7] certain sub-sectors do offer opportunities for mutual benefits from bringing two good businesses under one roof.

Leveraging network benefits – such as a larger or more comprehensive distribution network – is another common characteristic of successful acquisitions. One excellent example of a company that does this effectively is Diageo, the consumer goods company with a portfolio of world-famous beverages. Often, Diageo's acquisitions not only add good but under-penetrated brands to the global portfolio – such as Zacapa rum, now part of its Reserve line; they also improve distribution into new markets for existing brands. Recently acquired brands from deals such as Mey Icki in Turkey and Ypióca in Brazil are now sold elsewhere and, more importantly, Diageo's existing brands are now selling better in both those countries.

ASSA ABLOY: QUALITY DEALS

ASSA ABLOY, the global leader in locks and door opening solutions, commands brands and businesses dating back four centuries. The Chubb brand, for example, was founded in 1818 in Wolverhampton, England and served a prestigious clientele that included the Duke of Wellington, the Bank of England, and the General Post Office for installation in all the country's iconic red Royal Mail boxes. The product of a merger in 1994, ASSA was founded in 1881 in Eskilstuna, Sweden and ABLOY in 1907 in Helsinki, Finland. Mergers and acquisitions have been a vital part of ASSA ABLOY's continued growth ever since.

During the late 1990s and early 2000s, ASSA ABLOY was a prodigious deal-maker as it consolidated a fragmented market. Since 2006, under the leadership of CEO Johan Molin, it has made over 120 acquisitions, primarily to expand geographical distribution and secondarily to deepen technological sophistication. During that period, the company added 8% annually to revenue so that today, nearly half the group's total revenue flows from businesses acquired under Mr. Molin. At the time of acquisition, businesses typically had lower operating margins, by as much as five percentage points. On integration, margins rose. Everything else being equal, acquisitions would have diluted group operating margins meaningfully, from 15% in 2006. Thanks to strategic savvy and exploiting synergies, margins instead rose to more than 16% in 2014.

In one illustrative acquisition, among the biggest, ASSA ABLOY in 2002 acquired Besam, the world leader in automated door systems. Until then, ASSA ABLOY lacked a substantial presence in that segment, but the company went on to make Besam the foundation of an even wider division dubbed Entrance Systems. This now amounts to one quarter of group sales. Broadly in line with its typical acquisition multiple, ASSA ABLOY paid 1.5 times sales. Since then, Besam's operating margins have increased substantially, delivering high earnings growth over the period and solid returns on the acquisition.

But most ASSA ABLOY acquisitions are small, simple and complementary, which are reasons why its roll-up strategy works despite the perils of this approach to business growth. Another factor is a tendency to buy private companies rather than public companies, often offering scope to professionalize manufacturing efficiency and processes – some targets had been operating at only 50% of production capacity.

ASSA ABLOY's decentralized structure eases integration and enables multiple deals to be coordinated simultaneously. Newly acquired businesses readily plug into the group's vast distribution network, know-how and innovation. ASSA ABLOY's production structures and processes undergo continuous rationalization in response to ongoing growth, evolving from traditional component manufacture towards low-cost outsourcing and automated assembly. This dynamism is apparent from the evolution of ASSA ABLOY's operations: since 2006, the company has closed 71 factories and 39 offices while converting another 84 factories to assembly plants.

Experience adds value. Making hundreds of acquisitions over several decades yields institutional knowledge and wisdom. The demonstrated ability to avoid overpaying and execute on integration promotes predictability and renders related forecasting more reliable. While allocating the bulk of corporate capital to acquisitions can destroy value, ASSA ABLOY shows that, executed well, it can create prosperity: its share price has risen six-fold in the past decade. Its rationale for growth through acquisitions persists: although it is twice the size of the industry's second-largest manufacturer, ASSA ABLOY still only commands just over 10% share of the global market.

Despite the potential benefits, acquisitions are risky, and none of the foregoing rationales is foolproof. There is considerable evidence to suggest that acquisitions are more likely to impair shareholder value than increase it. Even good businesses – including some we are invested in – have stumbled. Managers do not always provide investors with sufficient information to evaluate proposed acquisitions completely or objectively. They invariably provide projections that look compelling and business rationales that seem logical. But the possibility of an acquisition tends to excite managers and ignite optimism, so we interpret these presentations cautiously.

Red flags such as diversification, scale, and rapidity often accompany ill-fated acquisitions. We worry especially about acquisitions whereby companies are expanding into new areas: management's relative lack of expertise and a clumsy business fit usually prove costly. (We agree with the sense of Peter Lynch's word-minting: that much diversification is really *diworsification.*[8]) We are averse to 'scale for scale's sake', particularly when managerial bonuses are paid based on metrics linked to corporate size, such as absolute revenue or profit growth. And we become concerned when a company completes multiple large acquisitions in a relatively short time frame. This would always lead us to probe whether the deal-making is a response to deterioration of the underlying business.

DIVIDENDS AND BUYBACKS

Excess cash – funds a company does not need to reinvest in the business or to seize attractive opportunities – should be distributed to shareholders as dividends or share buybacks.

Managers have considerable discretion in this area of capital allocation, so we appreciate companies that clearly explain buyback and dividend policy in their disclosures. Too often, companies repurchase excessively during periods of economic expansion, when stock prices are high, and insufficiently during economic downturns, when prices are low. Both propensities reduce rather than build value, the first by giving away more than is received and the latter by depriving shareholders of cash when it is particularly valuable to them.

During the financial crisis of 2008-9, for example, companies generally reduced share buyback activity while maintaining dividend levels. Managers tended to hoard capital rather than use it to repurchase shares – a safer, if less valuable route – because everyone else was doing the same. This unwise buyback pattern occurs in all economic environments, not solely those in which the markets are experiencing financial distress. Research examining US stocks between 1984 and 2010 found that "actual repurchase investments underperform hypothetical investments that mechanically smooth repurchase dollars through time by approximately two percentage points per year on average."[9] We admire companies that are consistently able to repurchase their own shares advantageously, but as a rule, companies buy back shares when valuations are less favorable.

THE COSTS OF WORKING CAPITAL

Working capital refers to resources deployed short term to generate revenue: short-term assets such as inventory, less short-term liabilities such as accounts payable. While inventory and receivables eventually turn into cash, until then they are tied up in the production and sale process. Companies enjoy some offset because their suppliers likewise extend them credit, but most carry net-positive working capital. Among European companies, working capital represents approximately 16% of sales.[10] A company's overall working capital burden often reflects its bargaining power with other stakeholders: those positioned to dictate terms typically enjoy more attractive working capital profiles.

For companies that grow, associated costs of working capital rise. Growth means more money is stuck in transit as inventory or unpaid bills. If a company ties up 10% of incremental sales in net working capital, then a significant percentage of cash that could have landed in investors' pockets will not. The incremental working capital required for growth is critical as it reduces cash flow growth, and hence the company's value creation. So companies that tie up very little extra working capital with incremental sales tend to be more attractive.

Most companies must bear the costs of carrying at least some working capital. Those best-positioned to mitigate the money drain are those able to produce at low costs (less cash tied up as inventory) or to operate with rapid inventory and receivables turnover: they speed up the time it takes to produce and compress the time it takes to collect. In some rare and attractive cases, working capital is negative: capital is held rather than deployed, making for a benefit rather than a cost. The most common examples are industries that require prepayments, such as software and insurance.

B. Return on Capital

Return-on-capital metrics measure the effectiveness of a company's capital allocation decisions and are also arguably the best shorthand expression of its industrial positioning and competitive advantages.

Theoretically, returns on capital should equal the opportunity cost of capital. An industry or a company generating economic profit normally draws competition, and competitive pressure gradually erodes profitability to erase economic profit. Thus, in perfectly competitive markets, companies earn no economic profit. To achieve sustained high returns on capital requires possessing features that protect returns from competition; namely, competitive advantages. Identifying what these competitive advantages are and understanding their sustainability is an essential part of the quality investment process.

Quality investing focuses on a company's ability to invest capital at high rates of return: post-tax levels of high-teens (and higher) are possible. Three elements drive corporate cash return on investment: asset turns, profit margins and cash conversion. Asset turns measure how efficiently a company generates sales from additional assets, which can vary greatly depending on the asset intensity of the industry itself; margins reflect the benefits of those incremental sales; and cash conversion reflects a company's working capital intensity and the conservatism of its accounting policies. Before exploring each of these concepts below, we take a brief look at the challenge of measuring returns.

Returns

The simplest and most commonly used tool for measuring returns is return on equity: net income as a percentage of shareholders' equity. While useful as a general proxy, the figure is crude for two reasons. Most obviously, the return part of the equation uses accounting measures, whose application leaves managers with considerable discretion over the treatment of important measures such as depreciation and provisioning. The calculation can also be distorted by factors that affect the value of shareholders' equity, such as write-downs and debt levels. The latter is particularly problematic, since the leverage effect of debt boosts return on equity but does not reflect the associated risks: many of the failed financial institutions in the 2008 crisis boasted seductive returns on equity in preceding years.

Ultimately, return measures should illuminate the cash return from each dollar invested by a business, irrespective of capital structure and accounting techniques. Measures such as return on invested capital (measured as net after-tax operating profit divided by invested capital) go some way towards achieving this. Better yet is a metric zeroing in on cash returns on cash capital invested (CROCCI);[11] this is measured as after-tax cash earnings divided by capital invested after adjusting for accounting conventions such as amortization of goodwill. CROCCI measures the post-tax cash return on *all capital* a company has deployed.

These return metrics are snap-shots, measures at a moment in time, which can be distorted by, for example, cyclicality or the timing of an acquisition. An IRR (internal rate of return) calculation, such as Credit Suisse's CFROI[12] metric, addresses this point, but adds other complexities. Hence, we tend to use CFROI in conjunction with the other metrics we set out above.

Whatever one's preferred way to measure returns, the challenge remains that future incremental returns on capital may differ from historical returns on capital. While tempting to look at short-term incremental return as a proxy, this can be misleading. Often capital spent today will only deliver meaningful returns years later. Similarly, the returns a company achieves today may be the result of capital spent years ago, or a current cyclical boom. While history can never replace thorough analysis, we typically focus on companies where return on capital has been high and stable over time. Although studies suggest that abnormal returns tend to fade over time in aggregate, there are regular exceptions to this rule – outliers able to buck the statistical trend of mean reversion and sustain superior returns over the long term.[13]

ASSET TURNS

Asset turns are, in effect, a measure of a company's asset intensity. Or, put another way, how much capital needs to remain in the business in order to generate sales. Asset-light industries are attractive since they require less capital to be deployed in order to generate sales growth. The finest examples are franchise operations, such as Domino's Pizza, where growth is funded by franchisees rather than by the company. Other instances include software businesses, such as Dassault Systèmes, a leading European developer of design software.

One risk for low capital intensity business is attracting competition – evident in sectors such as online gambling, especially in Europe. Such companies must have additional competitive advantages that reduce this risk of new entrants: brand in the case of Domino's and intellectual property in the case of Dassault. However, high capital intensity companies can also be attractive, especially where the capital requirement confers stability and deters entrants.

PROFIT MARGINS

Carbonated beverages like Coca-Cola and Pepsi have long faced competition from private label alternatives. From a cost of goods perspective, all sodas have similar direct costs: water, carbonation, flavor, sugar, and container; even storage and shipping costs run parallel. If factors like brand and flavor did not matter, consumers would simply buy the cheapest on offer. While some do, many are willing to pay a premium for their favorite brand.

The price difference appears in the branded soda maker's higher gross margin. In effect, the company's marketing and other brand management investments are attributed a value by the consumer.

This might be called their Midas touch. Gross profit margin demonstrates competitive advantage: it is the purest expression of customer valuation of a product, clearly implying the premium buyers assign to a seller for having fashioned raw materials into a finished item and branding it.

Although gross margin is a partial function of a company's industry and high gross margins can reflect low asset intensity, sustained high gross profit margins relative to industry peers tends to indicate durable competitive advantage. Zeroing in on gross margins, as opposed to bottom line net income, also helps distinguish competitive advantage from managerial ability: bloated but short-term cost structures can reduce net income and disguise real long-term competitive advantages. High gross margins also confer other advantages: they can expand the scope for operating leverage, provide a buffer against rising raw material prices and provide the flexibility to drive growth through R&D or advertising and promotion.

The more incremental top-line revenue that ends up as bottom-line profit, the better. Suppose two rivals each grow revenue by a dollar. If it costs one of them ten cents to do so and the other 80 cents, the growth is clearly more valuable for the former. Businesses with high operating margins are typically stronger than those with lower ones.

Sustained margin expansion also signals strength. Big swings in operating margins can indicate that major cost components are outside of management's control, suggesting that caution be applied. A company that consistently achieves both high gross and high operating margins indicates a strong competitive advantage sustainable at tolerable cost.

C. MULTIPLE SOURCES OF GROWTH

Among the most challenging aspects of business analysis is assessing long-term growth prospects. Analysts put considerable time into predicting growth in the coming quarter or year, yet it is more important and more difficult to gauge potential rates of growth over the longer term. While devotees of growth investing hunt for companies predicted to grow sales frenetically – say 15% or more annually – we tend to focus on companies likely to deliver half or two thirds of that on a reliable basis over the long term.

It may seem an obvious statement, but the best businesses to own are those in which end markets are growing rather than shrinking. Absent market growth, competitors feel compelled to grab or increase market share through any means, including industry-destructive tactics like price discounts and promotions.

Opportunities for growth maximize the benefits derived from high returns on capital. Such opportunities can arise from market growth, either cyclical or structural, or through a firm grabbing share from rivals in existing markets or expanding geographically. The very best companies enjoy a diversified set of growth drivers through ingenuity in the design of products, pricing, and product mix.

GAINING MARKET SHARE

Growth through gaining market share has two things in its favor. First, it is independent of the economic climate – share gains can occur in good times and bad. Second, it is something over which the company itself has a degree of control. Some companies are able to deliver consistent market share gains through strategies such as compelling advertising campaigns, successful store roll-outs (as with H&M) or ongoing investment in distribution. Companies with a proven track record of steady accretion of market share can be highly attractive investments.

When analyzing share gains, understanding the source is important. Market shares in some industries fluctuate dramatically depending on relative pricing strategies and product innovations of participants. Market share gains represent the best pathway for growth if they happen in a consistent way and, ideally, in a market where the investor can identify a reliable share donator. But it does get more difficult as market share grows: obviously, the easiest to recruit customers move first. It also becomes less significant as a company's share grows: gaining 1% of a market doubles the reach of an existing holder of 1%, while such a gain would be modest for the holder of a 10% share (a 10% increase) and negligible for the market leader (only 2% growth for one commanding a 50% share).

GEOGRAPHIC EXPANSION

Sometimes, successful domestic businesses reach a point in their existing markets where gaining share becomes tougher and they turn their attention elsewhere. Geographic expansion is one of the most challenging strategies for businesses to implement. Failed attempts are legion and can prove damaging to the original franchise. But if a company has cracked the code in a handful of markets, it increases the odds that it can do so repeatedly. Unilever, the Anglo-Dutch consumer goods company, has been building great franchises in emerging markets for more than a century. As the Unilever model suggests, past success with geographic expansion can be a good indicator of future success.

UNILEVER: GEOGRAPHIC EXPANSION

Unilever boasts a vast portfolio of personal care, home, food and refreshment brands distributed in 190 countries. The company derives almost 60% of revenues from emerging markets and has deep heritage in those locales, thanks partly to Britain's historical influence over large swaths of the globe. Its geographic expansion continues today.

India is a good illustration. Since 1956, the minority shares of Unilever's Indian subsidiary, Hindustan Unilever (HUL), have been traded on India's stock exchanges. Sunlight soap was introduced there in 1888, with several other brands launched over the next 20 years. The combination of longevity and local management means that such brands are considered home-grown. Such affinity is a huge advantage over relative newcomer brands from other multinational companies.

Unilever's longevity has enabled high market share and allowed the company to develop an advantaged distribution system, a fact local competitors concede. HUL has direct coverage of more than *three million* outlets in India. Far surpassing any rival, it distributes an estimated two-thirds of its products directly to retailers, skipping the wholesaler. In addition, the company launched its Shakti program in 2001 designed to promote business in rural India while extending HUL's distribution reach. The company boasts a sales network numbering more than 70,000 *Shakti Amma* (women) and 48,000 *Shaktimaan* (men) distributing Unilever products into rural villages – a huge sales force even for a country of India's continental scale.

The benefits of such a powerful distribution network are many. As well as delivering higher market share in less developed rural regions, it allows for a quick and astute read of consumer demand and preferences. Additionally, the company is able to launch new products faster and more broadly than its peers, leveraging its existing cost base more effectively. Success is evidenced by HUL's continued market share gains in India.

Beyond India, Unilever has been present in South Africa since 1891, Argentina since 1892, Thailand since 1908 and numerous other countries since the 1930s. By 1910, it had sourcing operations as far afield as the Pacific and West Africa. In terms of distribution, Unilever has matched, or is working to replicate, its Indian position in other markets from the outer reaches of Indonesia to sub-Saharan Africa. Even in these markets where

> networks are still expanding, the company's reach is impressive: Unilever's distribution network in Indonesia is bigger than that of the Indonesian postal system.

Companies that rely on unique business structures for competitive advantage at home will face the greatest difficulty expanding geographically. Advantages that derive from a unique distribution system, localized scale advantages, or favorable regulatory treatment may not be replicable abroad. The inability of grocery retailers, hospital operators, and airlines to globalize their businesses successfully testifies to this effect.

Conversely, certain types of competitive advantages travel better to new places than others. Thanks to the globalization of travel and media, premium brands transition relatively easily into new markets. Louis Vuitton and Nike are well-known in all corners of the world, even where their merchandise is not yet available. Manufacturers operating their own stores enjoy a particular advantage, as their vertical integration makes them less reliant on a country's infrastructure.

The uncertainty of geographic expansion leads us to prefer companies with proven track records of successfully exporting competitive advantages into new geographic areas.

PRICING, MIX AND VOLUME

Viewed from a purely financial perspective, growth in revenue can be broken down into price, product mix, and volume. Setting inflation aside, companies able to increase prices without corresponding increases in cost (or reduction in unit volume) have substantial pricing power. Such power is rare but extremely valuable because it is essentially cost-free: each dollar of price increase results in one dollar of pre-tax income. Pricing power exists when customers are insensitive to price increases. It may occur, for example, in brands whose high prices consumers take as ratification of quality or status (luxury items) and for products marketed on reputation when comparisons with alternatives are difficult ("farm fresh" or "organic" labeling).

A more common source of growth comes through price/mix optimization. For example, a boxed chocolate maker might mix into its standard package line a premium package and increase its price by more than its additional cost. As total revenues rise, the excess increases net income. Mix-driven growth is highly valuable, entailing limited capital expenditure and only modest increases in working capital. But it is inferior to pure price-driven growth because it usually requires some increase in production costs.

In purely financial terms, volume-based growth is the least valuable, since it entails increasing quantity at existing average unit prices. Incremental revenue from volume increases tends to have a minor impact on gross margin. But total costs, including those associated with the increases in working capital and capex that higher volumes entail, will inevitably rise to some extent as volume grows. As a result, volume growth is particularly valuable for asset-light businesses boasting high margins and those with high operating leverage, such as pharmaceutical or software companies.

CYCLICAL MARKET GROWTH

Cyclicality is a double-edged sword. Certain companies and industries tend to enjoy substantial growth during periods of economic expansion. Exact relationships vary widely across businesses and sectors; oil cycles tending to be long, agriculture cycles deep, and consumer cycles shallow. In any setting the potential for growth during cyclical expansions can be substantial, but the inverse is true when the cycle contracts.

Consider the hotel cycle in the US in recent years. Following a meaningful contraction of the business amid the financial crisis of 2008, there was a rebound in 2010 and cyclical expansion ensued. This has continued right up to the present. In real terms, revenue per available room, a standard industry gauge, rose sharply above the peak of the previous cyclical expansion. Earnings of major hotel companies grew in tandem. Marriott, for example, is set to deliver 2015 per-share earnings three times higher than those achieved at 2009's cyclical trough. From the nadir in early 2009 through late 2015, Marriot's share price rose nearly six-fold. An investment aligned with this cyclical upswing paid well.

However, cyclical growth poses analytical challenges: at some unpredictable point, a cyclical upswing reverses due to increased supply or reduced demand, at which point earnings and share prices tend to decline. In view of this, we focus on two things. First, we look for companies able to deliver real earnings growth through the cycle. Marriott and other leading hoteliers such as InterContinental Hotels Group are good examples: these companies gain share by adding rooms and benefit from a cycle that tends to show real growth from peak to peak. Second, we endeavor to understand the cycles that specific companies face as best we can, with a view toward avoiding downside risk while capitalizing on growth.

STRUCTURAL END-MARKET GROWTH

Whereas cyclical growth refers to episodic expansions, structural growth refers to more permanent expansions supported by persistent trends deemed likely to endure. The inherent prognosis, however, warrants skepticism, as the observed pattern is often in fact cyclical and merely temporary. Many emerging market trends previously considered structural seem, in hindsight, to have been more cyclical in nature.

Despite this, there are a number of long-term trends that are more likely to prove sustainable than others, ranging from disease prevention to urbanization and aging demographics in developed markets. But it is not safe to assume, for instance, that all people on earth want to own a certain number of cars or spend a stated portion of income on beer.

There are many examples of erroneous assumptions along these lines. A notable one occurred in the US golfing industry. Growth was projected to increase in tandem with a rising population, favorable demographics, and increasing wealth. The projection was wrong. Between 2006 and 2013, the number of golfers in the US fell by 18% despite 6% growth in the US population. A broader example is occurring in China, where once soaring consumer appetites for goods like cognac and pastimes like gambling have abruptly reversed. Only time will tell if this reversal is temporary or permanent.

The persistence of growth

Research undertaken over the past 50 years indicates that assuming historically high earnings growth will continue can be dangerous. A 1960s study by British economist I.M.D. Little[14] found no relationship between growth rates achieved by any given company in one five-year period and those achieved in the next five years. More recently, Credit Suisse's HOLT researchers found that, while sales and asset growth are weakly persistent, earnings growth is more random and uncorrelated with preceding years.[15] These researchers contend that the probability of a given company sustaining elevated earnings growth rates from one year to the next is negligible.

Given the philosophy we have outlined so far, such assertions are problematic. Are we kidding ourselves that we can have any insight into the growth part of the value-creation equation? When we do get it right, is it mere serendipity? We don't think so: here are some of the reasons.

Predicting earnings growth is a daunting task. Powerful evidence of the challenges in forecasting growth is the consistently poor track-record of equity analysts. During 2009-14, for example, these professionals overestimated earnings growth for the diverse European market (the Stoxx 600 index) by an average of more than 10% per annum![16]

Despite this backdrop, it is possible to produce reasonably accurate forecasts for a subset of companies that tend to generate more consistent and predictable growth than the broader market.[17] Even in the Credit Suisse study, a significant minority of companies maintain growth rates over the long term. The probability of this is greater for companies in the ten to 15% earnings growth range than in the higher, hyper-growth ranges.

A key part of the reason for this is the link with return on capital, which displays far greater persistence and is therefore a more reliable indicator of future growth. Consistent with studies carried out by Goldman Sachs,[18] Credit Suisse concludes that there is a relationship between higher CFROI and higher future earnings growth. We concur and believe that a stable, high returns profile is a good basis for better earnings growth predictability.

We know that chance plays a role in any prediction, but we disagree with the thesis that forecasting growth is entirely random. The stable, predictable medium-term earnings growth achieved by many of our portfolio companies supports our view that it is possible for well-positioned companies with high, stable returns to buck the overall statistical pattern.

D. GOOD MANAGEMENT

It is tempting to conflate the ideas of corporate quality and good management, but it is not always the case that quality companies have excellent management teams. On the other hand, the combination of strong management and a well-positioned company can be powerful. While a full treatise on the subject of management is beyond the scope of this book, a few key aspects warrant mention. Above all, good managers are disciplined stewards of shareholder capital. We start by explaining what this means in practice, before assessing a few other good managerial traits, such as tenacity and candor.

DISCIPLINED STEWARDS

Good managers have the patience and discipline to invest in organic growth and the willpower to resist the temptation of a dash for growth through 'transformational' (and often value-destructive) acquisitions. Excessively proud management teams indulging in undisciplined acquisition sprees rarely create value for investors. Another sign of strong long-term thinking is a prudent balance sheet and counter-cyclical investment. Exceptional managers minimize borrowing and turn a recession into an advantage. For example, during the last downturn, H&M accelerated its store roll-out to take advantage of lower rents and better locations. Likewise, the Swedish bank, Svenska Handelsbanken, accelerated expansion of its UK branch network just after the financial crisis of 2008 when rivals were severely weakened.

INDEPENDENT, LONG TERM, AND TENACIOUS

Handelsbanken also illustrates how good managers are independent-minded – acting according to prudent conviction despite prevailing winds or consensus sentiment. The Swedish bank contradicts prevalent practices at peer financial institutions: it boasts a decentralized management structure, uses a profit-sharing plan rather than banker bonuses, and embraces a risk aversion that discourages proprietary trading. These traits enabled the bank not only to weather the 2008 financial crisis but to be a supplier of capital during the period. Of course, this kind of independent thinking is easier in companies with dominant shareholders or family control, features that insulate against pressure from both rivals and stock markets.

Good managers have long-term vision for a business and the tenacity to realize it. The history of Rolls-Royce's civil aerospace division illustrates the point. After privatization in 1987, Rolls-Royce stuck with its hugely expensive development of Trent engines for wide-bodied aircraft. Under two successive chief executives throughout the 1990s, the company's vision sought first to sell more engines and then to generate recurring revenue through TotalCare, an ongoing service offering that is priced based on an engine's hours in operation.

While some short-term shareholders criticized the strategy for its costs during implementation, long-term shareholders have gained enormously from the managerial vision and persistence. The Trent engines and related TotalCare have delivered significant value with the promise of more as Rolls-Royce transformed from a manufacturer into a more service-oriented business.

Good managers are never satisfied, but are instead driven by an indefatigable and passionate quest for improvement. Energy is devoted to relentless identification and eradication of potential threats. For example, Atlas Copco, the global leader in industrial compressors and underground mining equipment that operates in 180 countries, perceived a threat from potential low-cost Chinese manufacturers in its compressor business. To preempt the challenge, Atlas Copco established its own low-end compressor business in

China, in a bid not only to add profits, but to gain direct and accurate knowledge of the upstarts, the better to outflank them.

OUT OF THE LIMELIGHT

Shareholders should be wary of any company whose chief executive is portrayed in the media as a business celebrity. In their article 'Superstar CEOs', economists Ulrike Malmendier and Geoffrey Tate investigated the effect of celebrity status – proxied by the receipt of business awards – on company performance. They found that "award-winning CEOs subsequently under-perform both relative to their prior performance and relative to a sample of non-winning CEOs… They spend more time on public and private activities… The incidence of earnings management increases after winning awards."[19] We therefore generally prefer executives who keep a low profile. Nonetheless, fame sometimes benefits a company. Ryanair's CEO Michael O'Leary, for instance, sometimes courts the media glare in shrewdly calculated moves to generate free advertising.

PEOPLE MATTER

Good management recognizes that a top priority is developing and deploying people who will then help achieve an organization's goals. Some corporate cultures are famous for producing great managers. In the US, for example, at least 26 former General Electric executives became chief executive at other large companies while at least 18 IBM executives have become such leaders.[20] In Europe, at least four former executives of Atlas Copco went on to lead other major companies, including Alfa Laval, ASSA ABLOY, Munters, and Wärtsilä. While training and grooming practices vary, at Atlas Copco the practice is to rotate executives every three years through a series of roles to expose them to multiple perspectives on the business.

CANDOR

Good management extends beyond internal execution to outside constituents. From the investing perspective, that means effectively communicating to investors what is important and why. It also means being candid and speaking in a straightforward professional manner rather than indulging in the elliptical spin politicians favor. It also means speaking directly and honestly about events, not wrapping a message in prose developed by a public relations or corporate communications team. These traits should be on display in all settings, from formal periodic reports to occasional in-person meetings and regular earnings calls.

A NOTE OF CAUTION

While good management can enhance results from quality companies, success or failure is not invariably a function of managerial action. Outstanding results do not necessarily reflect outstanding management. In his eye-opening book *The Halo Effect*, Phil Rosenzweig argues that business narratives tend to exaggerate the impact of leadership style and management practices:

> "Much of our thinking about company performance is shaped by the halo effect, which is the tendency to make specific evaluations based on a general impression. When a company is growing and profitable, we tend to infer that it has a brilliant strategy, a visionary CEO, motivated people, and a vibrant culture. When performance falters, we're quick to say the strategy was misguided, the CEO became arrogant, the people were complacent, and the culture stodgy."[21]

Corporate performance is determined by many factors which defy tidy isolation. While good management and quality companies often seem to go hand-in-hand, and assessing managerial quality is indeed worthwhile, other factors such as industry structure loom larger. We turn now to this topic.

E. Industry Structure

The structure of a given company's industry is critical to its potential as a quality investment. Competitors will always toil to take away any excess return a business is earning. Knowing the competition and understanding how it behaves is therefore vital to assessing the durability of competitive advantage. Perhaps more crucially, over time some industries lend themselves to sustainable high returns for all players, even amid competition. These are situations when the overall industry and market structure neutralizes some of the usual constraints of economic theory. Good examples occur amid mini and partial monopolies, which we discuss at the start of this section. We follow this by assessing several other factors that can affect the attractiveness of an industry's structure including barriers to entry.

Mini-monopolies

From a perspective of economic attractiveness, being an unregulated monopoly is arguably the highest level of existence in the corporate world. If achieved, profits and returns are maximally strong. It is easy to think of big market structures when talking about monopolies, like Microsoft in operating systems in the late 20th century and Standard Oil in energy in the late 19th century. Real monopolies tend to be sizeable, rare, and disliked by governments. Focusing exclusively on monopolies would leave a small portfolio – along with considerable regulatory risk under a variety of antitrust laws worldwide.

Instead, when thinking about monopolies, we think small, in terms of what we call *mini-monopolies*. Mini-monopolies are about the real choices customers have at the time of decision rather than theoretical choices. They usually arise from a product offering highly-valued customer benefits unavailable from rival goods. That they exist more in customers' minds than in economic models means they are sometimes less obvious, but their financial characteristics can be compelling.

Take tobacco. We do not invest in the tobacco industry for ethical reasons, but it illustrates mini-monopolistic characteristics. Few people would argue that the tobacco industry is a monopoly: it may be concentrated, but competition prevails. For the individual nicotine addict, however, a favored brand occupies a unique position. A smoker almost always sticks to the first brand they smoked and, if a store doesn't carry this brand, will more likely go elsewhere than choose an alternative brand, even at a much lower price.[22] With such a loyal customer base, a monopoly is established. The main competition the tobacco company faces is in making the product attractive for new users. The extreme value of these mini-monopolies is one of the reasons why tobacco companies continue to make a lot of money despite extensive government restrictions worldwide.

There are many other examples of mini-monopolies but few are as extreme as tobacco. If a piece of equipment needs repair, the manufacturer often has a monopoly on spare parts. That is why they are expensive. Software upgrades and maintenance contracts typically sell at a high price compared to the cost of production. When a company makes products that yield unique customer benefits, it creates some sort of mini-monopoly. The degree is a function of customer loyalty – profound in the case of the hooked smoker and of varying intensity elsewhere. A company's degree of monopoly power also varies between existing customers, where loyalty is a historical legacy, and attracting new ones, which requires considerably greater ongoing investment. Finally, any given company may enjoy mini-monopoly power in some of its product lines but not in others. These groups deserve further analysis as they may contain some underappreciated gems.

PARTIAL MONOPOLIES

Broken competition occurs when competition exists in part of the marketplace but not all of it. The most common form of broken competition is localized supremacy: where a company enjoys dominance in some regions, but not others. Consequently, assessing market share on a country-by-country basis is often more illuminating than looking at aggregate global market share figures. Take the beer industry. Ambev's stellar EBITDA margins in Brazil – comfortably over 50% – reflect its insuperable position in that market,[23] itself a function of significant logistical barriers to entry. Contrast with Heineken, which, despite enjoying leading positions in many countries in Western Europe, generally faces at least one other strong competitor in each location. The result is a materially lower margin profile than Ambev.

Another form of broken competition is linked to switching costs. This occurs when a customer buying one upfront product, such as a razor or a software package, gives the producer something close to a monopoly by purchasing additional products such as replacement razor cartridges or software upgrades. For some companies, the economics of partial monopoly are so compelling that there is greater value in the back-end than the front-end.

The extent of the attraction depends on competition for the sale of the upfront product. If the upfront market is highly competitive, then much of the back-end monopoly profit subsidizes the upfront purchase. Consider cell phone service providers, where front-end competition led most to give cell phones to users for free, becoming a 100% customer acquisition cost. Contrast this with the compressor market. In addition to excellent service margins, market leader Atlas Copco also achieves solid margins on original equipment sales. The combination has allowed Atlas to sustain high returns on capital and strong operating margins for many years, despite the cyclicality of its end markets. We evaluate evidence of partial monopolies in terms of such different outcomes and try to assess specific reasons why an industry may develop along the cell phone model or the compressor model.

OLIGOPOLIES

Industrial economics 101 teaches that the fewer competitors there are in a market, the better it is for producers. It is a true statement up to a point: on a statistical basis, industries do get more profitable with higher concentration. But the broad averages obscure the fact that many industries are outliers and multiple rivals do not always impair performance. What determines whether industry concentration leads to a good or a bad outcome is, in our opinion, circumstantial.[24]

Consider two of the world's most famous duopolies: Coca-Cola and Pepsi in soft drinks; and Airbus and Boeing in aircraft manufacturing. The nature of their businesses is vastly different. Coca-Cola and Pepsi sell branded, fast-moving consumer goods. Airbus and Boeing develop high-technology equipment with long lead times. Even when it comes to market share, the pairs differ. Coca-Cola clearly dominates over Pepsi, while Boeing and Airbus share their market pretty evenly. In the aircraft business pricing is opaque, whereas in soft drinks it is far more transparent. It would not necessarily be obvious from these descriptions, but the margins and returns generated by the soft drink manufacturers have been meaningfully superior to those in the aircraft market.

Clues as to the relative attractiveness of the two industries appear by probing who the customers are and how the selling is done. In contrast to the soft drinks industry, the aircraft industry sells to a concentrated industrial customer base and every individual sale is negotiated hard. This puts pressure on pricing and, ultimately, industry profitability. In any sector, it is important to assess whether competition is as real at the micro-level as it appears at the macro-level. Sometimes what seems to be a competitive market is rather a latticework of smaller monopoly-like structures where all participants extract high profits.

Consider the differences between duopolies and oligopolies. When a company only has one competitor, it quickly becomes a corporate lightning rod. It can easily become a corporate obsession to beat the other company all the time. A case in point: the intense rivalry between Airbus and Boeing which contributes to the relatively poor economics in that industry.

Add a few more competitors – make the market an oligopoly – and participants often think differently. Beating multiple competitors all of the time is impossible, so companies tend to focus on fighting weaker competitors whilst leaving the stronger ones alone. Such an environment prevailed for years in the hearing aid market, and this ultimately resulted in the two dominant makers – Sonova and William Demant – consistently taking share from weaker competitors.

As a general rule, an oligopoly is preferable to a fragmented and volatile competitive landscape. On top of that, we look for oligopolies where the industry structure has been relatively stable over time and where the logic persists for that stability being maintained. Finally, we tend to prefer the leading players in oligopolistic markets – especially in industries where competitive advantages in areas such as R&D and A&P are enhanced by market leadership.

BARRIERS TO ENTRY AND RATIONALITY

Some industries or products are more likely to come under competitive attack than others. If an industry has many new players popping up all the time, beware: barriers to entry are low. However, industries with low barriers to entry may still have high barriers to success and scale – just look at the restaurant industry.

Still, a regular flow of new small entrants can destroy economics. By the law of large numbers, the sheer frequency of new entrants can eventually lead to one of them becoming successful and disruptive. In industries with high innovation rates, like healthcare and technology, this is a prevalent feature. The consequence is that larger firms must often spend substantial sums acquiring upstarts just to maintain their competitive position.

The fact that an industry has few or no new entrants is usually a good sign. It indicates that barriers to entry are high and tends to lead to more rational competition. Observing many older players in the industry is also encouraging – it's a sign that long-term survival is possible.

In some rare cases, the big firms in an old industry are still owned by the families that founded them. If this is the case, it is a good indication that the industry is not only enduring, but offers organic growth through retained earnings rather than dilutive new issuances of equity. The global confectionary industry is a good illustration. Of the six major firms, two are privately held (Mars and Ferrero); two are controlled by founding families or their foundations (Lindt and Hershey); and two are part of large conglomerates (Nestlé and Mondelēz).

RATIONALITY MECHANISMS

Understanding the potential consequences of disruption in a given industry is an important step in the process of assessing its attractiveness. In many industries, small price wars and market share battles will occasionally erupt. We try to assess whether these eruptions are likely to create all-out war, destroying industry profitability, or be resolved amicably. Given the inevitable risk of any given company in any industry behaving destructively, we prefer companies in industries with the ability to snap back to rationality and stability.

The best industries are those where all companies can afford to think long term. If an industry's technologies, demand and participants will remain constant, it reduces the incentive to attempt to increase earnings in the short run at the expense of the long. These kinds of effects tend to be more powerful if key industry players are family owned. While CEOs might have a three- to five-year perspective on a company, families think in generations. While bursts of irrationality undoubtedly arise in family businesses, they tend to be more contained. (We expand on the benefits of family ownership when we discuss corporate culture in Chapter Two.)

It also helps when the payoff from aggression is deferred. Take the case of partial monopolies, where upfront sales generate long-term monopolistic profit streams. When the cost of slashing prices today will take years to recover through future monopoly profits, rivals have less incentive for doing so. Similarly, it is advantageous if companies have a way to hit back at competitors through a tit-for-tat strategy: this is one reason pricing remains relatively rational in many parts of the household goods sector.

Disruptions to the marketplace can be long-lived and damaging if companies peg their assessments of success to achieving certain levels of market share. This is particularly an issue in industries where scale is important to success. When players in an industry see losing share as a systemic risk, aggressive pricing may seem rational, despite the damage it can do to overall industry economics.

While customers are quick to embrace price cuts, they fight price increases. It can take years for the impact of price wars to diminish. The real danger from poor pricing discipline arises when it changes customer behavior or expectations. With branded products, discounting is the most common way to do this.

Discounting can be seductive in the short term: it boosts sales, enables companies to hit their profit targets, and even brings gains in market share. But it is dangerously addictive. When companies see that it works once, they are often tempted to do it again. Competitors typically follow suit to protect market share and the industry starts teaching customers to expect persistent discounting. Once that occurs, the industry has trapped itself.

Such behavior eroded profitability in the laundry detergents category. Having taught consumers to buy in bulk on sale is also one of the reasons why Coca-Cola struggles with profitability in North America. We appreciate company policy to avoid discounts, as this is a sign of a genuinely long-term view as opposed to seeking artificial short-term boosts that risk long-term performance. LVMH's Moët & Chandon, for example, did not discount its champagne during the global financial crisis that began in 2008, despite a sharp contraction in demand. Instead, the company opted to build inventory, which it ultimately sold at full price when the good times returned.

THE ADVANTAGE OF SHARE DONATORS

When we study industry participants, we look to see if there are any particularly weak members, whom we call share donators. These are businesses that help rivals by ceding market share and profits on a recurring basis. Amid the ebb and flow of most industries, we occasionally see clear patterns of share donators. The most common sources are management incompetence and suboptimal product mixes, but both of those can usually be corrected within short time frames, so we don't count on them as long-term sources of gain to industry leaders.

The more sustainable share donators suffer from structural problems. Ignored divisions of large companies, which are provided with fewer resources and mediocre managers, cede market share; a good example was Siemens' hearing aid business (now in private equity hands).[25] Another category includes smaller companies unable to scale up as an industry consolidates or globalizes – although not all of these surrender share routinely or readily. In Germany, for example, despite global consolidation of industries from paint to beer, markets remain fragmented and competitive thanks to tenacious family-run mid-size firms.

Other share donators are companies with entrenched cost or management structures that impair adaptability. The airline industry provided many examples: older airlines shackled by legacy costs, aging fleets, and the old hub-and-spoke business model fell prey to low-cost airlines delivering much cheaper point-to-point travel. Obviously, having sizable share donators among competitors does not in itself make a company great, but the advantage is worth analyzing and can add value to quality companies that are able to capitalize on it.

To assess the likely future stability of a given industry, we will always look at its history. Markets where industry dynamics have been substantially unchanged and competition relatively rational over many years are more likely to remain that way. Another, more subjective, assessment we make is of competitive rhetoric. Where companies talk about peers in respectful terms, the competitive behavior often reflects this. If the language used is dismissive or aggressive, the risk of mutually destructive behavior increases.

Security by obscurity

In business, as in nature, the ability to keep out of sight of potential predators is an advantage. While locks, lenses, ostomy products[26] and bathroom fittings all play an important role in everyday life, they occupy humble corporate niches. These sectors are relatively small, are not experiencing hyper-growth and do not offer obvious opportunities for technological revolution. We believe that this relative obscurity can offer a layer of protection from competitive disruption.

Financial and intellectual capital is drawn towards ideas that can change the world and which have the potential to make big money fast. Consequently fields such as renewable energy, robotics, electric vehicles and disease prevention garner disproportionate focus. You are less likely to see vast amounts of capital allocated to improving ostomy bags or gaining share in the toilet fittings market. While operating in a niche sector does not, in itself, make a company great, it can help. An obscure industry, even one with appealing economic characteristics, tends to face lower disruption risk, making attractive industry structures more durable.

F. Customer Benefits

The products of quality companies confer considerable benefits on their customers and understanding the relative value of these benefits is an important part of business analysis. We focus on a few types of benefits most likely to differentiate a product or service in a way that yields superior economics. After introducing each – intangible benefits, assurance benefits and convenience benefits – we consider how different customer types respond to them.

Intangible benefits

Intangible benefits arise when product decisions are made based on benefits that elude easy measurement. People have a favorite soda primarily because they enjoy the specific taste. Similarly, high-end handbags are not bought for utility but because of the image they project. Factors like taste and image are tough to measure objectively, but offer considerable intangible consumer benefits. With purchases based on intangible benefits, price is usually secondary.

Intangible consumer benefits tend to be more prevalent in smaller items or those considered an indulgence. Think of your decision-making when buying chocolates for your partner on Valentine's Day. Price is probably not among the most important factors. If the ticket price is larger, tangible and rational benefits tend to play a bigger role. This explains why many people buy their favorite candy without checking price but might spend hours online researching the best deal for a car.

Intangible benefits often matter more to customers the more intimate the products are. Products that go in the mouth or on the skin carry more intangible potential than those that sit on a table or go into a machine, explaining why most people give the cost of their preferred toothpaste less thought than the price and brand of dishwasher detergent. This is one of the reasons why certain consumer products companies, from edibles to cosmetics, have proven to be such strong businesses over time.

L'ORÉAL: THE BEAUTY OF INTANGIBLES

Vanity is venerable: ancient civilizations as diverse as the Egyptians, Chinese, Indians, Japanese, Greeks and Romans used scented oils, mineral pastes, and natural dyes to mask body odor, paint skin, and dye hair. Catering to these deep-seated impulses, today's cosmetics industry generates revenue of nearly $250 billion. Purveyors sell "hope in a jar," as Revlon founder Charles Revson once put it, including some pricey products, such as the $2,000 price tag for Estée Lauder's Crème de la Mer moisturizer.

The market leader is L'Oréal, founded in Paris in 1909 by a young chemist named Eugène Schueller, whose strong brands translate consumer appetite for beauty into significant pricing power. It is adept at exploiting the lack of a direct link between price and outcome or between price and input cost. A small tub of Lancôme Visionnaire anti-wrinkle face cream, for example, retails for $90, five times that of mass-market rival offerings such as Nivea.

Consumers are unlikely ever to test the comparative effects of the two products and no consumer can compare results of using any given product with results of not using it. So relatively small perceived advantages can be hugely valuable. And L'Oréal nurtures customer trust in its brands and an emotional connection with them as intimate products – applied to eyes, lips, and other sensitive areas. Pricing power arises from intangibles that are often unquantifiable, unlike what is necessary to gain pricing power for commercial and industrial products.

While consumers of many goods, from automobiles to snacks, can only consume so much, the scope for consumption of cosmetics is almost limitless. A recent study, for instance, showed that the average Korean woman uses 11 beauty products and spends 40 minutes every day on her beauty regime. Few sectors offer such scope to sell more products to existing customers. Many consumer surveys indicate that the beauty regime is among the last to be cut even when times are tight.[27] That is why the cosmetics market has proven to be less discretionary than one might imagine: demand rises during economic expansions and tends to remain steady during contractions.

L'Oréal attracts customers by offering a wide line of cosmetics products and dominates across channels, price points, categories, countries and brands. It typically gains share in each, demonstrating sustained consumer trust, which is driven by two primary strengths. The first is the scientific basis for its products, achieved thanks to enormous scale and the effectiveness of its R&D program. L'Oréal has been responsible for introducing a high proportion of new chemicals into the industry, many remaining critical components of its products today. The second is getting the information to consumers: the company is the world's third largest advertiser, notable because the two largest – the diversified consumer products giants Procter & Gamble and Unilever – have more numerous product lines.

L'Oréal's pricing power manifests in its high gross margins, which exceed 70%. Combined with strong cash generation, good returns on capital and a steady top-line growth trajectory, such compelling margins complete a virtuous circle which has enabled the company to sustain its market leadership. Success is longstanding and shared with owners: L'Oréal boasts regular dividend increases stretching back over 50 years – with a 16% compounded annual growth rate over the past 14 years.

ASSURANCE BENEFITS

If shopping for a parachute, the chances are you would care about one thing above all else; that it worked. If offered a parachute selling for a fraction of the price but with greater risk of malfunctioning, you would be extremely unlikely to take up the offer. The impact of failure would be perceived to be too large to be worth it.

Many consumer products pose the parachute scenario. Another company may offer a lower cost option, but the consequences of failure are seen as devastating so consumers will pay more for products such as child safety equipment, life jackets, bicycle helmets, and fire alarms, to name a few. For customers, the value of knowing – or believing – that they are choosing the most reliable or highest quality product can translate into a highly sustainable willingness to pay a premium price.

Consider the assurance effect in the context of manufacturing processes. If the failure of a small machine or input component can cause the shutdown of a manufacturing plant, customers will work with only one or two suppliers. While customers know that this will result in a higher cost, they are willing to pay extra for reliability. Suppliers of industrial gases such as oxygen, hydrogen and carbon dioxide illustrate the point: while such gases are scarcely proprietary, they have a few peculiar characteristics that give their suppliers an edge. They constitute a small cost of many manufacturing processes but are expensive to store in large quantities. If supplies are disrupted, entire chemical plants and refineries are forced to close, causing substantial economic loss. The upshot? A new low-cost provider with no reputation will often lose to a higher cost provider with a good track record.

Assurance benefits also appear in many settings outside of manufacturing. When parents buy baby food, a well-known brand like Nestlé's Gerber provides assurance that the food is healthy and safe. Companies pay a premium to use well-known product-testing or auditing firms – such as the Big Four – both as an internal assurance benefit and because it offers assurance to stakeholders. Farmers pay a premium for tractors from manufacturers such as John Deere because they offer time-tested quality products, fearing the risk of equipment failure on harvest results.

Assurance benefits are often based on reputation. A reputation of high quality or reliability is earned over time. To compete with reputation is almost impossible, no matter how much money is staked on it.

SGS AND INTERTEK: WHEN IT PAYS TO BE SURE

Consumers buy goods with expectations that will they meet certain standards. Beef buyers expect merchantable food and purchasers of home appliances expect effective performance. Consumer willingness to pay, which defines the seller's pricing power, is directly related to a product's expected quality. Pricing power can be sustained only if customer expectations are consistently met.

Yet modern vendors face two challenges. On one hand, supply chains are growing longer and more complex. In previous eras, manufacturers controlled much of their production process but today they outsource a great deal, often to remote outposts around the globe. Producers must still vouch for their product but have far less control over the inputs. On the other hand, consumers and regulators alike are growing more circumspect, demanding greater corporate accountability. Technology broadcasts failures around the world so that product problems are rarely local any more.

To address the challenge of reduced information about production processes combined with the increasing costs of deviation from standards, producers are increasingly turning to testing services. These are impartial qualified referees who provide product assurance, offering a seal of approval that customers value. Much like traditional auditors and rating agencies, testing companies such as Bureau Veritas, Intertek, and SGS have for more than a century staked their reputations on such product, commodity, asset and process certifications. Testing companies with strong reputations can charge clients more, as producers buy a sign of confidence in product quality. But even for premium testing services, such assurance remains a negligible component of overall product costs.

Testers boasting global capabilities command both stronger reputations among clients and greater pricing power, making scale a barrier to entry. Scale can also improve institutional knowledge, speed turnaround times and drive the unit cost of testing down. Testing services become an attractive alternative to conducting in-house testing. Often, clients also need to allow testing companies to integrate into their information technology and operations platforms. The considerable fixed upfront costs this entails tend to lock producers into engaging and retaining only two or three nominated testing services, rather than multiple rivals competing for the business. These traits manifest in the economic results of global testing service companies, some of which enjoy margins exceeding 30% and hefty returns on capital in their consumer goods testing businesses.

CONVENIENCE BENEFITS

Simply making a product readily accessible is an easy way to provide a clear benefit to customers. This can be best thought of as a convenience benefit. In its most basic form, consider neighborhood grocery stores and restaurants. They may not offer the cheapest or tastiest food, but neighbors pay for proximity. A benefit based solely on geography, however, is vulnerable to competition, as it does nothing to prevent new rivals from moving in nearby. Likewise, there is an advantage to being the sole state or regional product distributor, but it too may be transient as the value proposition remains based on a forced choice by the customer.

A variation on the convenience theme is customer intimacy. This refers to sales models that position companies to best serve customer needs by offering convenience and efficiency. The principal source of customer intimacy is a direct relationship with existing customers – incumbency. A strong sales force can provide such a benefit, which is especially valuable for complex products where the salesperson assumes the role of advisor. Intertwining products with personal affairs also helps, as when bank customers adopt automatic payroll deposits and bill payments or when telecommunications customers bundle cable, internet, and phone products.

CUSTOMER TYPES

Customers are diverse but it pays to distinguish between two broad groups: retail consumers and corporate clients. Retail consumers can be fickle, acutely price-sensitive on some items and spendthrift on others. While marketing experts devote endless time to studying these varying proclivities, one thing seems clear: consumers are more willing to splurge on items offering intangible benefits, particularly for smaller purchases.

Business customers vary widely, especially in size, and small companies can be more like consumers, generally inclined to cost-consciousness but occasionally willing to pay up for intangible or convenience benefits. As a rule, the larger a company is, the more objective its purchasing decisions; it will focus on direct cost savings increases and the willingness to pay for intangible or convenience benefits decreases. In addition, large corporations increasingly use procurement departments that enhance rational behavior in corporate buying.

This does not mean corporations are not attractive customers, but that it requires deeper analysis to assess a supplier's ability to extract value from the sale. A few rules of thumb emerge. First, buying corporations pay the greatest attention to high-priced transactions involving contracts made at the highest levels in the organization. Companies can sell large numbers of lower-priced goods to corporate customers where purchase orders are made and approved without significant involvement of senior managers or the general counsel's office. Second, sellers tend to fare least well on products sold to corporations through bidding processes or organized negotiations where extensive product comparisons spell intense competition among suppliers that drives price down. Above all, the more a corporate decision is driven by price rather than other factors, the less attractive it is from a seller's viewpoint.

Corporate buyers are generally more receptive than retail consumers to the concept of 'total cost of ownership'. A machine that provides reliability and/or measurable production cost savings can be priced to reflect such benefits. Similarly, corporations frequently embed the products of certain suppliers in their manufacturing processes. Given the size and complexity of many corporations, the cost of changing suppliers can be significantly higher than simply the cost of product. Software is a great illustration: while there are cheaper alternatives to SAP, it dominates partly because customers know that switching is painful and expensive, in terms both of direct cost and business disruption.

Corporate risk aversion is a powerful trait for sellers to exploit. In large corporations, making significant mistakes gets both individuals and the entity as a whole into the deepest trouble. As the famous 1980s saying goes: "No one ever got fired for buying IBM." Similar to the case of retail customers, the prevalence of risk aversion among corporate buyers gives a clear advantage to products sold for their quality assurance benefits.

G. Competitive Advantage

The operator of the sole ice cream stand on the beach has a unique competitive advantage: it is a functional monopoly, the only purveyor of the product in that market. But this particular competitive advantage is hard to translate into further growth. The ice cream vendor might be able to increase revenues through price hikes, or by improved product mix, but the advantage is not scalable – there is no guarantee of being the sole licensee on any new beaches.

The competitive advantages we seek can create economic moats in the same way as the ice cream seller's monopoly, but have the added benefit of being replicable. Competitive advantage is a broad topic and is integral to all the patterns we examine in the chapter that follows. Here, we highlight three aspects of the subject to set the stage: technology, network effects, and distribution advantages.

Technology

The most important facet of competitive advantage derived through technology is sustainability. A product offering superior benefits for customers will have a competitive advantage and should yield above-average economic returns, but having just one product in this category is usually insufficient to sustain a competitive advantage. Rest assured, a superior product will quickly be copied. In mobile phone handsets, it typically only takes one or two quarters before all major players copy attractive innovations. While patent protection isolates a firm from some pressure, it is only a partial and temporary offset, as the pharmaceutical industry illustrates: drug prices collapse by 80-90% when patents expire.

When considering technology as a competitive advantage, the first question is magnitude. For some companies, technological edge is so slight or fleeting that it scarcely constitutes a competitive advantage. If the technology advantage is significant enough, the next question is how a company can keep churning out better technology than its competitors. Technology is only a sustainable competitive advantage if it helps make products that deliver superior customer benefits over long periods of time.

The simplest route is outspending rivals on R&D. Scale can also build barriers to entry that deter smaller rivals. Examples include inherent technological complexity; a need for advanced or interdisciplinary research skills that are harder to assemble and coordinate; and exorbitant capital costs for research equipment. But innovation is not only a spend game. A diverse set of innovation opportunities helps to mitigate the risk of total disruption across product lines – lose one race, win others. A low profile that avoids attracting interest from outside the sector or from competing non-traditional competitors such as governments or academic institutions is another plus.

R&D is frequently viewed as rewarding the swiftest, stoking a frenetic research pace. But since longevity is a more durable competitive edge, the race is more often won by the surest rather than the fleetest. When the pace of research is more measured, development typically unfolds in small increments and through relatively complex improvements. The company tweaks a number of variables to gain marginal product improvements. Since incremental innovation is usually complex, it is more reliant on deep product knowledge that further entrenches long-established industry members: leaders stay in the lead.

Take jet aircraft engines. After years of rapid innovations from its invention during World War II until the late 1960s, the basic design was largely optimized. Since then, improvements have come from incremental changes in materials, coatings, and design. Given product complexity, large research teams were required to achieve the increments, with simultaneous testing for unintended side-effects:

a small change in one component can adversely affect another. The cumulative gains over many decades have been substantial increases in fuel efficiency.[28] Not a revolution but a huge gain for end users, as airline fuel costs amount to one-third of total expenses.

For products such as these with long lead times, market leaders can harness incremental innovation to deter new competitors. Even supposing that a brilliant and well-financed innovator could perfect a new engine with 10% greater fuel efficiency, getting it to market would take years. Over that period, incumbents would slowly catch up to close the gap on fuel efficiency, eclipsing the start-up. Moreover, jet engines are often sold at an upfront loss in order to generate service revenue – adding yet more years for new entrants to recover costs.

Advantages in data collection and manipulation can often produce powerful competitive advantages. For Google, user data is endlessly harvested to refine algorithms that improve internet search performance. Another example is the credit-scoring models of Experian, which are continuously updated with new data to deliver superior products that reinforce the competitive advantage over rivals.

While technology can be a powerful and profitable competitive advantage when it works, it remains a challenging edge to sustain. A quick glance through the history of technological dominance should prove the point, from Kodak and Polaroid to telephone answering systems and fax machines. Only a handful of companies have maintained technological leadership over time. Many faded into obscurity as the competition caught up or the direction of technological development shifted.

SYNGENTA: TECHNOLOGY ADVANTAGE

Syngenta was formed in 2000 by combining the Novartis and AstraZeneca agribusinesses, with roots traceable to the 1930s. It is today's global market leader in crop protection and among the top three players in seeds. Its peer group includes Bayer, BASF, Dow, DuPont, and Monsanto. Syngenta has the broadest crop presence in the industry including Corn, Soybean, Specialty Crops and Cereals. Given the continually rising global demand for efficiently produced food, Syngenta is exposed to a compelling long-term dynamic.

In the agribusiness, innovation is crucial. Without ongoing investment in the development of novel chemistry, rivals will grab market share. The scale and complexity of required R&D creates an entry barrier to smaller rivals, one reinforced by the considerable time required to develop and commercialize innovation in agricultural products.

The cost to research, develop and launch just one new active ingredient can reach as much as $300 million and the process may take up to ten years. Given the scale, product range, expertise, and patience required to succeed, new entrants would incur substantially higher costs while not recovering the investment for many years.

Syngenta ranks amongst the largest investors of the sector in R&D – some $4 billion over the past three years alone. Payoffs are considerable. Product launches from 2011 through 2014 are estimated to have peak sales potential of some $2.7 billion, and the pipeline beyond this could contribute a further $4 billion. These outcomes attest to how an innovative product pipeline supports sales growth.

The company's innovation responds to farmers' needs. For example, Latin American farmers faced enormous pressure from late season crop diseases, such as rust disease. Syngenta has a longstanding leading position in this market and recently invested to develop a new fungicide, Solatenol, to fight rust. Farmers welcomed the product, which achieved first-year sales of $300 million in Brazil alone, making it the largest product launch since the creation of the company, with a forecasted peak sales potential of $1 billion. Such figures show that breakthrough innovation can yield considerable return on investment.

Syngenta can be responsive to customer needs by innovating with new mixtures that draw on existing resources to improve current products while experimenting to create products to address new challenges. Solatenol, for example, is combined with another existing product, Amistar (azoxystrobin), to produce Elatus for use specifically on soybeans.

Syngenta illustrates how a business exposed to cycles can still prosper during downturns. Although farmer incomes are linked to crop prices, farmers continue to plant fields and protect crops in almost any economic environment. While farmers readily cut purchases of tractors and other capital equipment during cyclical troughs, they tend to curtail the frequency of crop protection sprays more modestly. For Syngenta, this relatively stable environment supports the capacity for sustained long-term innovation.

Rising global demand for food from population growth and wealth increases cannot be met by increasing acreage but requires increasing the yields from existing acreage, which means innovation for greater agricultural efficiency. Syngenta is poised to contribute this vital and valuable innovation. Leading in crop protection, with 20% of the global market and with a strong position in seed technology, Syngenta's unique portfolio of assets and strong culture of innovation position it well to maintain its attractive and stable long-term returns on capital.

NETWORK EFFECTS

Network effects arise when a system's value increases as more people use it. In most cases, network effects represent a tangible benefit to customers, as with social media sites. An auction site is a classic example of a business benefiting from network effects. More sellers offering products attract more buyers, which entices more sellers and so on in a compounding circle. Other examples are classified ad forums and stock exchanges. Internet search is another, though with a twist: the generation of data that enables the refinement of search algorithms keeps drawing in more users who in turn leave more data for endless harvesting and refinement.

Ironically, when network effects are too strong, they may backfire. An extremely efficient network can produce monopoly power and government intervention risk rises. As much as network effects are to a consumer's benefit, a monopoly isn't. Other stakeholders and users can also turn against a company that is perceived to be too dominant. In the case of online housing portals in the UK, an alliance of real estate agents has coordinated to form a rival, onthemarket.com, to compete against dominant players Rightmove and Zoopla; although the impact of this disruptive new entrant is currently unclear.

Another area of concern is the high pace of innovation in many areas where network effects are particularly prevalent. While it is easy to spot the benefit of network effects, networks face potential disruption that can be sudden and devastating. In social media, Facebook unilaterally killed several network businesses, including MySpace and MSN Chat.

Distribution

Distribution as a competitive advantage means that a company's route to consumers is more effective than its rivals' for an otherwise equivalent product. For manufacturers who distribute through middlemen rather than making direct sales, relationships are critical. The best manufacturers nurture these relationships to make them mutually advantageous. Such relationships often provide a significant layer of protection for manufacturers.

Think of a scenario where a store feels the manufacturer treats it well, that customers like the product and product sales contribute meaningfully to the store's profit. It would take considerably more than a cheaper price from a rival manufacturer to induce the retailer to switch or alter its product mix. Rivals can offer lower prices, but a retailer faces risks: the relationship with the new manufacturer may not turn out as well or customers may like the alternative less.

Distribution as a competitive advantage changes form when dealing with large chains where procurement is more rational. While relationships still matter, the laws of economics determine the competitive advantage. Large retailers know their size and value to manufacturers. Consequently, they will bargain firmly, pitting manufacturers against each other, even dropping those who won't negotiate. In this case, having exceptionally strong product offerings that customers really want matters greatly.

When a company's ability to service or fix a product is vital to customers, distribution can take on a critical role. The need for a service network creates a chicken-and-egg challenge for manufacturers. If customers don't buy a product unless they know it will get serviced, companies may have to invest in a service network in order to sell. Having a service network running at low utilization, however, is expensive. Consequently competing against companies with established service networks can be daunting, as it requires significant upfront costs. If such costs are high enough, they deter competitors.

* * *

We have, so far, looked at industry structures and competitive advantages in isolation, but each one of them is a building block towards corporate excellence. Identifying, or even constructing, a quality company would be simple if these building blocks were all uniform – but the reality is much more complex.

The long-term financial outcome for business is determined by how these different blocks fit together. There is no set template for success. Sometimes an apparently beautiful edifice can be built on very shaky foundations – something we discuss in more detail in Chapter Three. Conversely, short-term vagaries can mask the solidity of other corporate structures. In the chapter that follows, we highlight some of the configurations that, in our experience, have proven most enduring; the patterns that are most likely to be signifiers of quality.

CHAPTER TWO
PATTERNS

WHEN LOOKING FOR QUALITY COMPANIES, the desired outcome is always clear: strong, predictable cash generation; sustainably high returns on capital; and attractive growth opportunities. Yet the building blocks that enable companies to achieve these results vary widely, given the diversity of industries, business models, and competitive conditions. This richness of opportunity prevents us from articulating strict rules or rigid definitions of quality investing. Rather, a comprehensive probe reveals that quality companies achieve that status through many different routes.

Examine these routes, however, and patterns emerge: similar combinations of strategies, techniques, or capabilities that transcend companies or industries, like pricing power or brand strength. Some of these patterns assume more subtle shapes, such as ongoing service revenue of manufacturers of such diverse products as elevators and software, or supportive intermediaries in industries as different as plumbing, dentistry and ostomy products.

These patterns help to explain how different companies achieve the specific economic targets we seek. Although many of the patterns overlap, few, if any, companies exhibit all of them; indeed, for many businesses one is enough. All the patterns are tools an investor can use to guide business analysis in the hunt for quality. In this chapter, we present a dozen patterns, starting with recurring revenue.

A. Recurring Revenue

Recurring revenues arise when an existing customer base buys additional services or products from a company: jet engines requiring service, security systems with trailing surveillance and response, and periodicals with subscription renewals. The most powerful version arises when such obligations to pay for the service are locked in. For instance, a customer who has already purchased equipment or software from the company is likely to require additional purchases from the provider in the future. The installed base of equipment then becomes an in-house monopoly with consistent revenue streams for the producer of the equipment. It becomes a virtuous circle for the company: the larger the installed base, the bigger the monopoly, and the more predictable the revenue streams.

High degrees of recurring revenues increase the stability of a business and the predictability of its cash flows. Such benefits even hold true for companies operating in cyclical industries. Take elevators, for instance. Equipment sales fluctuate in tandem with new construction, an inherently cyclical business. But service revenue continues steadily through economic downturns as building owners, occupants, and governments put a premium on safety and reliability. Even as new installations fluctuate, the existence of an installed base makes revenue growth relatively predictable. Such stability can be very valuable to investors. It yields predictable business models for value creation even in industries exposed to the volatility of cycles.

Product upfront

Most recurring revenue models need an upfront sale to close before kicking in. While strong recurring revenue with upfront sales frequently converges towards an attractive industry structure, it is not inevitable. If a company struggles to generate new upfront sales at poor returns, related costs eat into the gains of ensuing recurring revenues.

But if a company enjoys competitive advantages on the front-end as well as the recurring revenue, the economics of the business are doubly strong. The most notable examples of this are software companies like SAP and Microsoft in the late 1990s and early 2000s. This was before the emergence of cloud computing, where recurring revenues remain but not necessarily with any upfront payments. There can also be a benefit to the challenging economics of upfront sales. It virtually shuts out new entrants. To build an installed base takes time. A new entrant may suffer years of losses before enjoying gains from aftermarket revenues.

The other potential downside to the lock-in effect of upfront selling is that resulting monopoly dynamics are known to customers and suppliers. Suppliers may price related inputs higher and customers may press harder for upfront price concessions. Low margins will reflect these costs and must be assessed against the superior economics of the subsequent recurring revenue.

The license model

The purest form of recurring revenue involves periodic licensing fees that follow upfront product purchases. This license model features prominently in the software industry, where customers first pay an upfront installation charge and subsequently make monthly or annual payments for maintenance, support and upgrades. While customers may opt out of the license fee, most opt in, because without it there is substantial risk of product inoperability or obsolescence.

THE SERVICE MODEL

Outside the software industry, the more common form of recurring revenue is the service model: when repair, maintenance, and overhaul revenue can be expected on products sold but whose timing and extent are more uncertain. Many industrial companies enjoy good service revenue streams linked to products sold, but it is not always automatic.

Corporate purchasers of capital equipment have several maintenance and service options other than their original equipment manufacturer, including rivals and third-party service companies. In some cases, even spare parts can be sourced from third parties. To make the service model work, therefore, companies must successfully compete against such alternatives, meaning converting new equipment sales into service contracts.

The best result is a portfolio of long-term service contracts with large customers who pay a fixed annual fee. An exquisite example concerns jet engine manufacturers. They often enter into sizable multiyear total care contracts with large airline customers to have engines serviced and parts replaced.

Such results are most likely for manufacturers whose products are critical to customers – such as jet engines. Aircraft engine malfunction midway across the Atlantic poses the gravest consequences. The more significant the results of breakdown, the more likely owners are to buy original spare parts and purchase service contracts offered by the manufacturer.

Service models are strengthened when the risk of damage from product disruptions are regulated or mandated by law. Although laws can change, their existence reflects heightened risks that concern all customers. Government regulation comes into play with such products as elevators.

Another source of strength for the service model arises when the breakdown of a piece of equipment is likely to cause economic disruptions for its owner. Ship engines are a good example. Having a ship docked for lengthy service periods is extremely costly to its owner. Ship owners are therefore likely to put a premium on regular service and speed of repairs. Wärtsilä, a Finnish company with leading positions in the marine power and energy segments, excels in this area due to the breadth of its extensive service network.[29]

Product longevity influences the value created by the service model of recurring revenue. The longer equipment remains in use, the longer it will require service and spare parts. Equipment with a useful life of two or three years tends to be replaced rather than repaired on breakdown; costlier and longer-lived equipment is more often upgraded rather than replaced.

Longevity has an offset, of course. Well-made long-lived equipment rarely breaks down and some machines will last decades with no or little specialized maintenance. The issue is how much annual recurring revenue can be expected, as a percentage of upfront annual sales. The bigger the percentage and the lengthier the time span, the better.

SUBSCRIPTIONS

Subscription services are a form of recurring revenue that leap to mind when thinking about this economic feature of businesses, but it is probably the least rewarding form. The installed base is not upfront product purchases, but existing subscriptions where the recurring revenue resides in prospects for subscription renewals.

That difference requires attention to the lock-in mechanism's strength. Some services offered on subscription-like terms are undifferentiated, such as a cell phone plan. When the cost of switching is low, customers soon migrate to cheaper options. In this business model, the dominant competitive dynamic is to become the low-cost producer rather than to exploit the value of recurring revenue.

Subscriptions that are either differentiated or embedded into an automated system can be attractive. A differentiated subscription is when a company's product lacks close rivals: a good example might be periodicals with genuinely differentiated content, such as *The Economist*. An embedded subscription exists when a provider transmits information which is incorporated into larger systems or processes, such as pricing data transmitted to market analysts or credit histories sent to bank credit scoring personnel.

DENSITY AND NETWORK BENEFITS

Service businesses benefit from growing their installed base in numerous ways aside from direct growth in sales and service revenue. Density economics contribute value: the more installed equipment in a region, the more efficient its maintenance becomes. Service personnel spend less time travelling between sites and have more experience with local environmental effects on equipment. The greater the density, the lower the cost of recurring revenues and, therefore, the greater the profit.

Network effects add value: the larger the service network, the faster it can meet customer needs, especially high speed of repair. Consider the farmer whose tractor breaks down mid-harvest. Swift repair is vital and the manufacturer with a nearby service center will get the job done more speedily. When shopping for equipment initially and evaluating after-purchase service arrangements, such businesses consider proximity a selling point. A larger service network is able to provide it.

ECONOMIC EFFECTS

In most recurring revenue models, customers fund a provider's business: customers pay ahead of delivery of goods or services. Many such companies can operate with negative working capital, meaning fewer resources are tied up in operations, which translates into lower costs and higher profits. Indeed, for most other companies, growth in size entails greater costs of working capital; for those enjoying recurring revenues, growth can instead drive greater benefits from working capital.

Subscription and service revenues tend to be billed in advance. Revenue therefore turns into cash more quickly than for companies that bill and collect only after goods are delivered or services rendered. Cash is always more valuable the earlier it is received.

Subscription and service revenue tends to require little capital investment to support growth. At one extreme, software companies update product files at the flip of a switch; even manufacturing companies typically produce spare parts using machinery and equipment already in operation. Specific service activity is also asset-light – usually personnel and a simple set of tools.

The combination of potentially negative working capital, rapid cash flows, and low capital expenditure to support growth is rare in business – but is a common feature of the recurring revenue model.

Many companies enjoy some degree of recurring revenue and many managers strive to increase that component of overall operations, but a small amount of recurring revenue does not necessarily make a company great. Rather, for the pattern to warrant serious consideration as a signifier of quality, recurring revenues should be an overriding feature of the economics of the business – a trait we see in companies as seemingly diverse as Atlas Copco, Dassault Systèmes, Rolls-Royce and KONE.

KONE: RECURRING REVENUES

Elevators are one of those ubiquitous, everyday objects people take for granted – except when they malfunction. Although modern elevators may be faster and smarter than the originals invented in the 1850s, the basic technology remains unchanged. Whether you walk into a century old elevator in Paris or a brand new one in Shanghai, the basic concept – motors and hoists – is the same.

Founded in Helsinki, Finland, in 1910, KONE started life as a machine shop repairing electric motors. Transformation into a global elevator business began in 1924, when KONE was acquired by the Herlin family, which still controls the business. In the 1960s, under the leadership of Pekka Herlin, a flamboyant character with a diligent work ethic, the business leapt forward through a number of judicious acquisitions.

Today, thanks to continued organic growth as well as savvy deal-making, KONE is among the world's largest elevator companies. Together with ThyssenKrupp, Schindler (also still controlled by the founding family) and Otis Elevators, they control nearly 70% of the global elevator market.

While elevator sales generate considerable revenue, when KONE makes a sale, it is equally focused on ensuing service revenues. After all, elevators last for generations, making many of those who purchase them one-time buyers, but they must be serviced in perpetuity. Unlike many products, servicing elevators is not discretionary. Since accidents can be fatal, most governments mandate elevator maintenance and building owners and their insurers would likely insist on making the investment anyway.

The margin on the upfront sale can be low, but sales typically secure years of annuity-like service revenue at a high margin and high return on capital (the 'attach rate' for KONE in developed markets is more than 90%). Service margins are so strong that participants keep them confidential, but a good estimate would put them at well over 30% in many markets.

Strong margins are due in part to pricing power conferred by customer preference for having the original manufacturer provide maintenance. Density economics fortify margins, since the more elevators placed in a given area, the more efficient the service organization. Small rivals can scarcely compete.

Given KONE's large base of installed elevators, recurring maintenance and upgrade revenues comprise just under half of its revenues, and a far greater portion of profit. With every new elevator installed, the service business expands, thereby growing the recurring revenue base. As a result, overall business profitability is remarkably consistent, despite the cyclicality of the construction activity.

A good illustration occurred during the deep recession stoked by the financial crisis of 2008. Despite a sharp decline in new elevator orders for a few years, KONE boasted a 13% compound annual growth rate in earnings from 2007 to 2010; in its worst year of the period, 2009, earnings were merely flat, not down.

Service fees are usually paid for upfront, making KONE's one of those rare businesses with negative working capital. The payoff is a high and steady return on capital. The strong returns, coupled with growth through both market share gains and an expanding market, is powerful. Over the past decade, KONE has more than doubled its top line and nearly quadrupled its bottom line. The performance has made it the most valuable company on the Helsinki stock exchange.

B. Friendly Middlemen

Many businesses must deal with middlemen to reach end consumers. The middleman's role can be positive or negative on a company's growth, margins, and returns. In trying to understand the varying roles and results, we have identified several useful patterns, pivoting around what we call the *friendly middleman*.

The helping hand

Among a company's more valuable middlemen are those that bundle delivery of the company's product with their own expert services. In one such type of bundling, the middleman is both a salesman and an expert, say a dentist recommending an implant or even a brand of toothpaste.

Or take an optometrist, who administers an eye test and prescribes glasses. Customers naturally ask for the optometrist's professional advice on the choice of lens and style. Unlike a salesperson at an electronics store, people are inclined to trust the optometrist despite the fact that he is also a salesman. Clientele are called patients, not customers. As a matter of professional training and reputational interest, the optometrist's goal is to deliver you a pair of lenses that fit your needs and make you happy.

As a matter of economics, the optometrist's goal is to maximize dollar margin by selling the most expensive pair of glasses that meet those professional criteria. Patient interests are often aligned – high quality is paramount and premium pricing is acceptable given the setting. (If a cheap pair of reading glasses would do, the scene would be a discount pharmacy where a customer plunks down $20 for a 1.5 magnification.) Thus a lens maker, such as Essilor, is in an attractive business position, benefitting from a professional expert whose incentives are to sell high-priced products that serve patient needs.

A second example of bundled delivery involves customers paying for the professional installation of manufactured products, for example by electrical or plumbing contractors. Customers tend to focus on the provider's hourly rate and minimize that rather than inspect brand offerings and haggle over those prices. Product safety and reliability, not cost, are paramount.

The craftsman's goals are not necessarily aligned with those of the customer: besides safety and reliability – after all, he will be blamed for failure – and perhaps ease of installation, his focus will not be price, except to the extent of helping his own margin, which will point towards the pricier end. The manufacturer is again in an attractive position: an expert chooses the product, while another person pays the bill.

LOCK-IN

Don't let the preceding discussion make you think that every company always benefits equally from having a third party choose the product while a different party pays the bill. There is considerable variation to the payoffs from this three-party pattern. The involvement of independent financial advisors or procurement consultants, for example, can complicate purchasing processes. These professionals sometimes function more as costly gatekeepers than friendly middlemen. The middleman needs reasons to recommend a company's product and companies employ various strategies to provide these.

One is product differentiation. The company distinguishes its product in terms of value either to the middleman or to the end user. The middleman must have a reason to endorse this product over another. Among expert middlemen, such as doctors or craftsmen, a reputation for product excellence and/or outstanding service will often suffice. Experts tend to take pride in their own professional reputations, which are best protected and enhanced by association with likewise reputable items. Reliable customer service is equally important, as the middleman takes the blame for product delays and malfunctions.

For complex products or those that are difficult to install or consume, professional training is a compelling lock-in strategy. If a third party provider is well trained in the installation of one company's product, chances are that they will stick to it and recommend to customers. As a bonus, training also serves as a barrier to entry: professionals weaned on a given product or technique face switching costs to learn how to handle rival offerings.

GEBERIT: FRIENDLY MIDDLEMEN

Geberit is the European leader in lavatory products such as toilet flushing systems and pipes. Founded in 1874 as a plumbing business in Rapperswil, Switzerland, it gained momentum a generation later when the founder's sons expanded into production of cisterns for flush toilets. Since then, related technology has evolved to put an ever-increasing portion of the plumbing behind walls, to save space and for a better look. Geberit hastened this trend with its 1964 introduction of the first concealed flushing cistern; it has sold more than 60 million since.

The behind-the-wall trend shifted industry focus from design to technology; it also made installation and repair more challenging. For bathroom builders and owners, once the aesthetics of such products were no longer relevant, choice became a function of reliability and price. In such circumstances, customers tend to rely on qualified experts – in this case, licensed plumbers. Geberit has made the plumbing trade its friendly middlemen.

As with end customers, plumbers seek quality products, ideally those that are easy to install and unlikely to break. Unlike end customers, however, plumbers are insensitive to price, because the end customer pays the bill. By nurturing strong relationships with plumbers, Geberit capitalizes on this gap between decision-makers (the plumbers) and end customers.

Aside from strengths rivals may pursue as keenly, like wide product availability and strong technical support, Geberit's tactics enrich its relationship-based strategy in several distinctive ways. Geberit provides plumbers and apprentices with free training on product installation, on-site if required. The program builds loyalty through product familiarity and saves plumbers the time and cost of apprentice schooling. In a typical year, Geberit's sales force might conduct 200,000 customer visits to plumbers, architects, and other target groups.

Furthermore, Geberit protects plumbers by stressing both ease of installation and lifetime reliability. This long-term product dependability enables Geberit to protect and promote plumber reputations.

To sustain these relationship commitments, Geberit invests substantially in R&D, with an annual budget exceeding $50 million. The investment helps develop products that respond to customer demands and to comply with changing building codes. For example, recent regulations in many locales mandate noise-reducing pipes for apartments and hotels, and Geberit makes compliant products that ease the burden – and risks of violations – for plumbers.

Geberit amplifies the value of these distinctive tactics by operating counter-cyclically. While rivals retreat during construction and renovation downturns, Geberit takes advantage of plumber downtime to increase training and loyalty-building efforts. The strategy delivers even during the downturn. For example, despite challenging economic conditions since 2006 in France, Geberit's sales have nearly doubled in this market.

Consistency and predictability are Geberit hallmarks, thanks to these strategies as well as an outstanding management team and corporate culture supporting them not only in production but across operations. Operating margins are high and grow steadily (from 14.6% in 2002 to 24% recently), with highly efficient working capital and significant pricing power (compounding at about 2% since 2002); return on capital is strong and rising consistently (from 14% in 2002 to 35% in 2014); and market share gains are reliable, with ten-year compounded annual volume growth of some 3.6% despite the contraction of the European construction market.

C. Toll Roads

Many large industries are served by niche suppliers whose services or products may represent a relatively immaterial proportion of that industry's cost base, but which are crucial to its successful operation. This position of being a small, but vital, cog helps to create significant barriers to entry; often meaning that suppliers' own competitive landscapes are oligopolistic and stable rather than broad-based and unpredictable. Good examples include companies in fields such as professional certification (auditing, rating agencies, product testing) and specialty ingredients (for products as diverse as yogurt or motor oil). Companies in such niches benefit by extracting part of the economics from every unit of volume in a larger, often relatively stable, industry. We call them *toll roads*.

Gold standards

There are certain companies that customers simply accept as the gold standard in an industry. A conspicuous example is the debt rating industry, where investors and regulators rely upon a handful of firms, dominated by Moody's Investors Service and Standard & Poor's Corporation, to rate bonds. They charge significant fees, paid by debt issuers, for ratings that simplify investor analysis. Also designed to bring order to credit markets, the industry's stability and related barriers to entry are illustrated by the fact that it survived, basically intact, despite considerable rating errors in the years leading up to the financial crisis of 2008.

Such independent verification or testing services operate in many settings, such as financial auditing, supply chain management, and consumer product reviews. They offer particular value when risks of error are high, both from the direct consequences of failure – such as misallocated capital or injuries – and from the second-order effects of harm to reputation or legal liability. Such services may have even greater value when used by third-parties rather than the payer, as with both bond rating agencies and financial auditing.

Globalization and increasingly complex supply chains stoke demand for independent verification. As companies source from more counterparts around the world and have operations in multiple jurisdictions, the value of global gold standards increases; a trend that has benefited the testing companies, SGS, Intertek and Bureau Veritas, as noted in the earlier case study.

Other gold standards originate in training. Many professions require members to use certain types of programs, from medical diagnostic equipment to engineering and architectural software. Training can be costly and repeated use increases knowledge and switching costs and promotes standardization.

In finance, the proliferation of Microsoft's Excel software illustrates an arc leading to the toll road: from school to basic training at firms to the corner suite, finance professionals and many people in other fields learn it, master it, and rely upon it. In engineering and architecture, the software used in universities becomes the software used in firms, yielding a self-reinforcing push for standardization: employers want well-trained students and universities want students who will be attractive in the job market.

Industries where educational training is paramount, therefore, are swiftly left with a narrow range of providers. Products become entrenched in educational programs, which leads to adoption outside academia. The embedding of these products in the workplace adds strength to the dynamic, because retraining an entire staff can be expensive.

MAGIC INGREDIENTS

Another area where toll road patterns appear concerns 'magic ingredients'. These are inputs bearing low cost but high value in production processes. Magic ingredients manifest in many settings. In the food and beverage industries, take enzymes, flavors and fragrances. For yogurt makers, starter cultures and flavor additives represent a small fraction of total cost. But they can have a material impact on the taste and texture of the final yogurt, which ultimately determine sales.

In industrial processes, gases have a similar role: the cost of oxygen used in steel mills is trifling but if supply is disrupted, production ceases. So companies tend to pay up for oxygen, preferring to buy only from the few big reputable companies that dominate this toll road.

CHR. HANSEN: THE POWER OF MAGIC INGREDIENTS

Calf-gut does not sound promising as a foundation for a successful global business. Yet, when Christian Hansen started out, its sole product was rennet: a complex of enzymes extracted from the fourth stomach of young ruminants, commonly used in cheese production. In 1874, the company's eponymous founder began commercially producing rennet from the premises of a former metal workshop in Copenhagen, Denmark. Overseas expansion followed quickly, with representatives selling Hansen's rennet across Europe and a powdered rennet factory opening in America.

Other products soon followed: natural colors for dairy products and starter cultures for foods like yogurt, butter, and sour cream. Technological advances also led to most coagulants being made with modern fermentation technology, not animal stomachs. Today, Chr. Hansen is the global leader in supplying cultures and enzymes to the food industry, which continues to account for the bulk of its business.

Next time you bite into a hunk of Gouda, you may (or may not) want to pause to reflect on the probability that it contains a blend of mesophilic and thermophilic culture strains: a typical Hansen product. Such starter cultures have several effects on cheese-making, as a catalyst for converting milk into cheese and releasing enzymes to enhance flavor during maturation. Traditional dairies keep their own cultures, retaining some from each batch for use in the next, but the result is often inconsistency. Chr. Hansen's cultures address this problem by providing a product that gives reliable outcomes time and again; greater consistency of flavor and texture and usually a superior product. Convincing traditionalist producers to convert to Chr. Hansen can take time, but once the switch is made, the relationship holds fast.

Several reasons explain this. For one, the absolute cost of Chr. Hansen's product is low. Cultures rarely account for more than 1% of a customer's input expense, paltry in relation to their effect, which can determine a product's commercial fate. Given the low price, potential savings from switching to a cheap competitor are negligible. Furthermore, cultures tangibly affect food flavor and texture. In yogurt, for instance, these features are integral determinants of customer appeal. Tinkering with a successful product formulation is risky. Finally, Hansen products usually improve customers' process efficiency, yielding cost savings on top of the addition of valuable consumer benefits at low cost.

Chr. Hansen's economics also benefit from scale. Biological production is a volume game, with larger batches generating higher margins. The company's global market share, at around 45%, enables it to invest in the largest state-of-the-art production facilities in its market. Competitors lack the throughput to justify comparable investment. Chr. Hansen's R&D budget is also unmatched in the industry and its effectiveness is amplified by its unparalleled library of biological strains, documented down to the genome. This powerful combination of deep embedded knowledge and continued research spending helps to enshrine Chr. Hansen's leading position and makes it highly unlikely that a new player will attempt to enter the market.

Hansen's enviable position as a critical, niche supplier to a large industry is reflected in its outstanding financial characteristics. In the latest financial year, operating margin exceeded 25%, return on invested capital was 35%, and sales growth was 8%. This is on a par with its annual achievements since its 2010 initial public offering. While many companies may proudly produce an essential consumer product, few offer customers such transformative value along with production gains at such a nugatory cost. Truly a 'magic ingredient'.

Industry structure and economics

Toll-road companies are typically oligopolies, not monopolies. While customers (and governments) perceive value from few producers versus innumerable rivals, a sole supplier presents a cost to competition that is too great to pay. Hence there are four global financial auditing firms, four industrial gas providers, three major credit rating agencies and three main testing companies. The lack of monopoly and substantial uniformity of products suggests that participants understand that they will be competing against each other for decades to come. That understanding leads to healthy competitive behavior rather than mutually destructive maneuvering.

D. LOW-PRICE PLUS

A strategy of undercutting the competition on price is rarely a durable competitive advantage, but when combined with enhancing features, the pattern can be compelling. We call this *low-price plus*. When price is the only thing that matters, a business is acutely vulnerable to competitive forces when rivals undercut. But some companies following a low-price strategy have succeeded spectacularly and quite a few could be considered quality companies. The phenomenal success in recent decades of the retailers IKEA, Inditex, and Costco attests to this. However, their pricing strategies alone do not explain either the success or durability of the model. Rather, the pattern combines low pricing with protection against the competitive vulnerability it creates.

LOW-PRICE BY NAME

Ask where to buy cheap but reasonable quality furniture and you will likely be told IKEA. Ask about affordable women's fashion and the names Primark, H&M and possibly Zara will crop up. When asked where to buy a cheap, quality pair of glasses, many Germans will likely mention Fielmann. Companies that can successfully forge a price-led model into a brand reputation for thrift go a long way to breaking the curse of low-cost vulnerability to competitive invasion.

The success of low-priced brands depends on several factors, the first being a degree of product differentiation. Consumers seeking affordable but decent fashion or decorative items that are less standardized (like jeans or sofas) will be influenced by factors such as fit and quality. So long as price is within budget, it is less likely that strict scrutiny will be applied to price, even if a cheaper sofa or pair of pants may be found down the street. Such price slack offsets the usual vulnerabilities for low-price-by-name business models.

The comparison between differentiated and commoditized products hints at a few conditions necessary for this achievement. Low-price-by-name offerings need to be both similar and different: IKEA furnishings must be fairly standardized but still distinctive. Playing off quality and differentiation lets companies create products that can be sold at attractive prices without giving customers the ability to establish whether it really is the best deal in town.

Yet while such low-price branding offers a first line of protection to the economic model, additional protection may be needed. This is because such branding only works as long as operators can keep offering customers what they want, which is a fair and attractive deal. Doing so is not easy – and therein lies the secret, and the second source of protection.

Scale is essential. Success entails obtaining thousands of inputs from around the world coordinated in a complex fashion, at considerable cost. The model depends on continuous and rapid response to shifting demand, meaning understanding changing consumer preferences, having control of the supply chain, managing inventory effectively, and deftness in distribution. All this requires good designers, operation mavens, and synchronized information technology.

Upstarts will struggle to do it all well. True, as technology and supply chain automation commoditizes, these business models may become more vulnerable. They nevertheless appear to have sustainable competitive advantages that protect against the vulnerabilities of the basic low-cost strategy.

LOW-COST SQUARED

A strategy of consistently low pricing is typically enabled by low unit costs. Some low-price businesses, however, achieve competitive advantages through several cost-saving small steps. When doing so translates into huge cumulative cost savings, the strategy punishes rivals and deters new entrants. We call this *low-cost squared*.

Many companies that pursue low production costs achieve lowest-cost status – for a time. The more routine low-cost tactics give only short-term advantages because they can be copied. For example, pallets – portable wooden packing platforms – were first used for stocking merchandise in deep-discount retailers but are now a common sight at many supermarkets. Low-cost airlines like Southwest pioneered shorter aircraft turnaround times, but traditional airliners soon followed suit.

In contrast, low-cost squared companies construct a business model, organization, and culture that drives low cost in each step of every process throughout the operation. The depth of cost consciousness adds protection that ordinary cost-minimization tactics do not. It is not the individual steps alone but their combination that creates the competitive advantage. Costs are contained everywhere, from sourcing and distribution, all the way through to employee travel budgets. We look for these numerous sources of pricing advantages; the more there are, the more competitors will struggle to replicate the net effect.

To illustrate how cost advantages consist of many small things added and squared, walk into a Costco store. Buildings are massive metal sheds in cheap suburban or rural locations. Lighting is cheap. Virtually all products sit on pallets – no shelving, stocking, or carting costs. There are no plastic bags. Stores only accept cash or Costco credit cards. While each saving may not account for much, in aggregate the cut is deep and lets the company do one thing and do it best: offer the lowest price.

Traditional retailers struggle to replicate all of Costco's advantages through frugality, though they copy what they can, like using pallets. Many are stuck in high-rent locales. Others invested considerably in display and presentation. Most opted long ago to accept alternative payment systems. Some have nowhere near the scale needed to challenge the Costco model.

RYANAIR: LOW-COST SQUARED

Ryanair started flying between London's Gatwick airport and Waterford, Ireland's fifth largest city, in 1985 with a single turbo-prop plane. Initially focused on the London-Ireland flight market, historically dominated by British Airways and Aer Lingus, the company spent the next 30 years muscling into markets across Europe route-by-route. Ryanair now operates 1,600 daily flights from 72 hubs, carrying more than 90 million passengers annually.

The bedrock of Ryanair's spectacular growth is being the lowest-cost provider – by a wide margin – in a legendarily inefficient and uneconomic industry. Ryanair exemplifies the benefits of substantial cost advantage: aside from fuel, Ryanair's unit cost is around half that of its closest competitor, easyJet, and far less than half of other rivals such as Norwegian and Air Berlin. Competitors must price fares at double Ryanair's rates, which explains why it continues to take market share across Europe.

Ryanair's low-cost strategy rests on extreme operating efficiency. Its greatest cost advantage is airport landing fees. Ryanair traditionally operated from smaller airports where it dominated airport owners, rather than the usual industry position of subservience. As a result, even when primary airports raise fees, Ryanair gets concessions. Its second biggest cost advantage is shrewd fleet acquisition. While other airlines, driven by pilot-focused cultures, prioritize diverse fleets of fancy aircraft, Ryanair built a uniform fleet opportunistically: in 2003, for example, amid an industry slump, it made a massive purchase of high quality Boeing 737-800s on the cheap. The bulk purchasing strategy also yields volume rebates from manufacturers and facilitates staffing an in-house maintenance crew, which is vastly cheaper than alternatives.

These two cost advantages are mutually-reinforcing, driving a deep and strengthening competitive advantage. The inexpensive planes allow Ryanair to fly profitably at low fares to small airports. Ryanair comes to dominate traffic at these airports and translates this dominance into significantly lower landing fees. A recent order to double its fleet over the next eight years will ensure continuity, perhaps acceleration, of these dynamics, as no other airline is growing as fast as Ryanair.

Ryanair is renowned for rethinking traditional aspects of European aviation and relentlessly finding ways to cut costs. Its ideas are often controversial, but rivals invariably follow suit to catch up on the savings. Examples from the long list are: charging for food and beverages; charging for luggage and airport check-in; discarding frequent-flier programs; and not using air bridges. Such bold moves also generate publicity, much of it critical, but this is then a cheap way to catch the attention of interested customers. As CEO Michael O'Leary explained:

"As long as you run around generating noise... it drives people on to our website. And we don't spend [hundreds of millions of dollars] on marketing companies to do it... Charging for toilets continues to be the number one story that resurfaces in the press and it's the gift that keeps on giving. We've never done it, but it keeps coming up on social networks every three or four months, the media picks up on it and then someone writes a story on it."[30]

Epitomizing the pattern of low-price plus, Ryanair continually leverages its competitive advantages. Of late it has used the profitability and leanness of its cost-consciousness to obtain aircraft acquisition financing at vastly lower rates than rivals, who must pay more due to costly structural burdens such as pension benefits. Similarly, Ryanair has begun to encroach into primary airports and business travel, to an extent replacing Europe's retrenching legacy carriers. Ryanair's cultural embrace of low-cost operation yields margins and returns on capital unrivalled in the industry. It boasts steady and substantial earnings growth with earnings tripling over the past decade.

BANKS: A FEW HIDDEN LOW-COST WINNERS

The banking sector is not generally a rich mine of quality businesses, but there may be a few hidden low-cost winners in the mix. As a sector, banking combines many elements we dislike: commodity products; high leverage; regulation and government support; and cyclicality. Operationally, gross margins of banks are expressed by net interest margin, the difference between the cost of funds (to depositors or others), and the price charged for funds (to borrowers). The margin is determined largely by uncontrollable macroeconomic conditions and available levers are often dangerous, such as charging too little interest or ignoring borrower credit risk. The latter poses an additional hidden cost: loan losses can sometimes take years to manifest. So banks can achieve high net interest margin, as well as high profit for years, not by being good bankers, but by being imprudent.

Accordingly, few banks pass muster as quality investments. The few that do might be called low-cost banks, such as Wells Fargo in the US and Svenska Handelsbanken in Europe. Thanks to their strong balance sheets, they can obtain cheap capital from deposits or, in Svenska's case, through unsecured bonds and other debt securities, and make high-quality loans with demonstrably low default risks. Lower cost of funding enables a bank to underwrite less risky loans and still make a healthy margin. Combined with low operating costs, a bank can deliver good returns with lower net interest margins. Epitomizing a low-cost culture, this series of features produce a self-reinforcing virtuous cycle.

Given the risks inherent to banking and the narrow zone of cost-consciousness necessary to qualify as a quality company, we stress corporate culture when evaluating banks. As the financial crisis of 2008 reminded everyone, the same banks seem to get into trouble repeatedly. It is unfair to blame management alone, as they come and go, but corporate culture, a more permanent feature, plays an important role in banking and other businesses. (We return to look at corporate culture in more detail later.)

E. PRICING POWER

Pricing power is a highly attractive feature: a company that can regularly raise prices above cost inflation is assured of growth, top-line and bottom. With no capital expenditure required to raise prices, enhanced returns on capital also result. The problem is that pricing power is often more conjectural than real – it is frequently discussed but rarely achieved.

SHADES OF GRAY

In an ideal world, a company with pricing power can raise prices significantly without any decline in volume. In reality, no company has such absolute pricing power. It is doubtful that any company could double prices without losing volume.

Pricing power can reflect the comparative perceived benefit of a product versus the next best alternative. However, the question is more often one of competitive structure rather than product type, as pricing power is typically held by monopolies or a mini-monopolies.

Indeed, many companies that have some degree of pricing power prefer not to discuss it due to its close association with monopolies. These companies are aware that the less that is known about pricing by customers, potential competitors and regulators, the better. A common way for companies to package the topic is to speak about price increases and feature enhancement at the same time, which tends to create less fuss with customers when higher bills arrive. In any event, as already discussed, the exercise of pricing power should be manifested in stable high gross margins as well as incremental periodic expansion in gross margin.

Pricing power derived from a standard monopoly structure is easy to spot, particularly if large or traditional. The most exquisite historical example, though now outdated thanks to the internet, was the only newspaper in town. While such classic monopolies do exist, companies with pricing power otherwise vary widely in their businesses characteristics. One recurring feature, however, is brand power.

HERMÈS: PRICING POWER

The elegant stores of Hermès occupy prime locations in major cities worldwide and the brand is synonymous with prestige. The company's origins are more commonplace, as its evocative logo hints. Thierry Hermès started the business as a harness and saddlery workshop in Paris in 1837. You can still buy a Hermès saddle today, along with a repertoire of celebrated products such as handbags, silk scarves, ties and perfumes. Nearly two centuries later, the business is still majority-owned and led by Thierry's descendants, who have imbued the current corporate culture with a transcendent long-term focus.

Now operating from over 300 shops, significant global expansion occurred under the long-term leadership of Jean-Louis Dumas-Hermès, who designed the Birkin bag after a brief encounter with the actress on a flight from Paris to London in 1984. As with all Hermès products, the Birkin bag is expensive and can cost you tens of thousands of dollars. At the lower end of the price range, silk ties will set you back $180. Throughout the product line, pricing is not only ultra-premium compared to ordinary brands, but also premium over other luxury brands.

What explains this pricing power? For one, product quality is exceptional. All the leather goods, nearly half of the total product line, are made in France by skilled craftsmen with years of training; other luxury brands increasingly outsource production of leather goods to low-cost countries. Some items, including Birkin and Kelly bags, are fabricated by a single artisan toiling for up to 20 hours per item. Whether leather or silk, only the finest materials are used, and the company has cultivated exclusive relationships with the best tanneries and silk merchants to secure supply.

Image is crucial. Hermès products are classically stylish, not modish. In fact, the company still uses saddle-stitching in its wares, a technique perfected in 1918 by the grandson of

Thierry Hermès when he launched a fine line of leather goods and luggage. To control brand image tightly, more than 80% of sales are made through company-owned stores in choice locations (the rest mostly made through international airport concessions). Exterior design and interior layout of the stores are an extension of the brand and a key point of communication with the consumer. Exceptional service levels are sustained through extensive training of sales associates.

Scarcity reinforces pricing power. Hermès invests in building production capacity, such as training new craftsmen, to support growth, but not to an extent that has fully eliminated bottlenecks. It is believed that there are waiting lists for some Hermès products open to regular customers. For some of the most desirable products, these waiting lists can be up to four years long. Pent-up demand results, which also deepens a relatively opaque – but very high – pricing structure. Many stores offer a unique assortment of goods, heightening a sense of urgency to buy. The genuine rarity of some items makes them collectors' items, such as a fuchsia crocodile Hermès Birkin bag that recently sold for $223,000 at a Christie's auction in Hong Kong.

Hermès has a high degree of control over the distribution of its products, thanks to its own-store network, giving it complete authority over pricing. Hermès products are almost never discounted. Price increases are common and always at least in line with general price inflation. The price elasticity of demand is negligible, reflecting the perverse fact that the more expensive a luxury item gets, the more desirable it can become.

The combination of these features gives Hermès unmatched pricing power. The benefits are reflected in Hermès' compelling financial characteristics: cash flows are strong and predictable thanks to operating margins exceeding 30%; return on invested capital exceeds 30%; the compound annual growth rate of sales during the past two decades is 11%, with the worst year in the period being 4% in 2009. The company's financial performance marks it exceptional, mirroring its heritage, history of creativity, and commitment to quality.

CONDITIONAL PRICING POWER

A common pricing pattern is what we call *conditional pricing power*: a company enjoying pockets of power due to select but recurring sales contexts. For example, an aircraft engine manufacturer may enjoy pricing power on its service business but this is conditional on its having closed a sale, where it may lack pricing power. Similarly, companies boasting loyal middlemen who impose effective monopolies likely enjoy a degree of pricing power. While far from uniform, conditional pricing power is more likely to be underappreciated by the market, making it of potentially great value to a quality investor.

PRICING FOR VALUE

Another form of pricing power exists when companies are able to price for value. In some cases, price-for-value increases are dubious exchanges but consumers nevertheless pay. The most conspicuous examples occur in the computer software industry, when vendors add small features accompanied by substantial price increases.

In other industries, price-for-value propositions are both more substantively meaningful to customers and less obvious to outsiders. Take seeds for farmers. Companies like Monsanto develop seed products that improve farm yields by 1-2% annually. Monsanto pursues a strategy of sharing the value upside with the farmer, raising prices each year to a level that means approximately one third of this benefit accrues to them, with the farmer getting the rest. A company that can continuously develop products while pricing for value can build durable pricing power.

THE DOWNSIDE: PRICE DEFLATION

Pricing power has a more sinister relative: price deflation. This often occurs in industries with substantial volume growth and significant innovation. It figures prominently, for example, in the technology hardware industry.

For some industries and during some periods, pricing deflation may be tolerable over the short and medium term when offset by increased volume or other gains such as operating efficiencies and declining equipment costs. But in the long run the economic prospects of such firms remain negative, as many companies in such industries ultimately fail. Although we know we may miss out on some potential long-term winners as a result, we tend to avoid investing in such industries.

F. Brand Strength

Not all strong brands are winners. In 1970, the US airline Pan Am was at its zenith. Its brand was one of the most recognized in the world, equated with glamour and adventure. This renowned brand did not guarantee superior long-term financial performance however: operating in a structurally challenging industry and buffeted by exogenous factors, the end came in 1991. From airlines to banking to newspapers and telecommunications, there are plenty of brands with superior name-recognition but inferior financial performance.

Being well-known is only one part of the equation. Successful brands also offer something differentiated, whether product, design, or image. Winning brands create an affinity, an attachment with the customer, either emotional or logical. For want of a better word, they are loved.

A company's industry plays a part: the Apple brand has its 'superfans', and there are life-long devotees of brands like Louis Vuitton, but we are not aware of similar appreciation groups for Air France or Delta Airlines – or Bank of America or HSBC. Differentiation and customer attachment allows for premium pricing and potentially gains in market share (the link between these two patterns and brand power is strong). Often such brands have non-replicable heritage and have endured over time.

Heritage: brands that improve with age

Some brands get better with age. Buy a Cartier necklace and you get both fine jewelry and a piece of history, following in the footsteps of European royalty. Ray-Ban Aviator sunglasses benefit from a tradition backed by movie stars and pilots over decades.

Such legacies are impossible to replicate: no amount of capital can reproduce such a history.

A further trait of many heritage brands is intertwining with specific geographies. Cognac, for example, may only originate in a certain region of France, by law. Sometimes the association is less direct, but no less powerful: Swiss chocolate sounds tastier than Finnish chocolate and leather goods from Italy or France are often perceived to be of higher quality.

TRUST AND CONSISTENCY

A brand is a promise; an implicit guarantee of qualities or characteristics. Sometimes these promises are bold (BMW: "The Ultimate Driving Machine"), sometimes more humble. Whatever it is, the promise needs to be honored consistently. The phenomenal global success of McDonald's is built on a simple formula: inexpensive food of consistent quality delivered quickly in a clean environment. Although McDonald's faces headwinds from increasing health focus in developed markets, its simple, unfailing formula drove unprecedented global success for a restaurant brand.

DIAGEO: BRAND STRENGTH

Diageo, born out of the 1997 merger of Guinness and Grand Metropolitan, may be a relatively modern beast but the portfolio of brands it controls has remarkable and enviable heritage. Many can trace their roots back to the 18th and 19th centuries. For example, Justerini & Brooks (J&B whisky) was founded in London in 1749 and in 1758 Arthur Guinness brewed his first batch of the black stuff at St. James' Gate in Dublin, which still produces Guinness to this day. Several of the Scotch distilleries were founded in the early 1800s, Lagavulin in 1816, and other brands like Tanqueray and Smirnoff date to the early-mid 1800s.

Most of these brands, headlined by Guinness, are stories of deep heritage plus savvy marketing that drives huge brand equity: enabling premium pricing and strong profitability. Just

---

one example of how this brand history can drive both volume and pricing growth can be found in Scotch whisky, Diageo's largest category in emerging markets and accounting for one third of its gross profits. Johnnie Walker is the company's most important Scotch brand and its heritage is central to its appeal. It was first shipped internationally in 1860 and won its first award in Australia in 1879. The famous square bottles were designed to make these early shipments easier.

The brand enjoys a significant competitive advantage due to this unrivalled international history. But antiquity alone does not sell whisky. To maximise its impact, the Johnnie Walker brand has been supported by considerable long-term investment at a level that simply would not be economic for a smaller brand. Diageo spends nearly $2.5 billion annually on advertising and is regularly acclaimed for the impact and vision of its promotions. The Keep Walking campaign for Johnnie Walker resonated with consumers and the brand has grown to become the global category leader in Scotch by volume and value.

In the Scotch market, time is Diageo's friend in another way as well. By definition, Scotch must be aged at least three years, in a barrel, in Scotland. Whisky matured for longer, often for more than a decade, commands premium pricing. Underlining this point, in 2014 Diageo released 160 bottles of Brora 40 Year Old, its most expensive single malt to date. The retail price? More than $10,000 per bottle.

This time requirement acts as a powerful barrier to entry. A new entrant wishing to sell aged whiskies must tie up huge amounts of capital before generating a dollar of revenue. And the necessity of intricate forethought to lay down inventory so far ahead of demand means supply is often constrained for older, more profitable Scotch. Consequently, Diageo's market share in all premium Scotch is approaching 50%. The combination of heritage, strong brand positioning and high barriers to entry confers impressive pricing power on Diageo's Scotch products. In recent years, Diageo has delivered a 6% compound annual growth in revenues per case of Scotch.

Diageo is the world leader in premium spirits, with market shares averaging around 30%. Relative to the competition, it boasts a wider spectrum of price-points across a more extensive range of categories, which makes Diageo the partner of choice for distributors and, ultimately, customers. Diageo's brands are often the first and most broadly available in a market. These features reinforce each other: good consumer access to the

> brands justifies further marketing investment; the scale of
> individual brands generates economies of scale in advertising;
> brand strength increases, allowing for better pricing; and scale
> builds with positive implications for cost efficiency.
>
> This virtuous circle magnifies the benefits of individual
> brand equity and helps to explain Diageo's high gross margins
> (consistently around 60%) and attractive operating margins (of
> around 30%). The irreplicable heritage of many of the company's
> brands provides a durable competitive advantage for these
> strong financial characteristics. We note with interest the recent
> comment from Diageo's CEO that Guinness is still only 256 years
> into a 9,000 year lease on its Dublin brewery: time is still on
> Diageo's side!

The danger of newness

In some industries, history is less important. Nintendo is one of
the most iconic brands in video gaming. Founded as a playing
card manufacturer in 1889, it produced its first video game in 1977
and owns video-game icons like Super Mario. Yet, before finding
partial redemption with its Wii product, it floundered. By the early
2000s, newer rivals such as Microsoft Xbox and Sony PlayStation
had overtaken it. The fact that Microsoft was only founded in 1981
or that PlayStation was launched in 1994 didn't matter. Superior
innovation from competitors diminished brand appeal.

The Nintendo case illustrates how brands are more vulnerable
when novelty and fast-changing technologies play a large role in the
benefits it offers. Innovation-driven vulnerability extends beyond
technology to affect many industries, such as the fast-changing world
of fashion. Innovation is a perennial challenge for apparel brands.

SCALE ADVANTAGE

Scale can be a crucial facet of a brand's success, providing advantages in marketing and distribution. In prestige cosmetics, companies like Estée Lauder and L'Oréal command large market shares. With associated high margins and capacity to spend on advertising and promotion, they can reach customers more easily than smaller rivals. In sporting goods, Nike can attack rivals posing a threat in a given market by immediately increasing exposure, even hiring the best local athletes to endorse products.

A similar dynamic holds for distribution. Scale enables a company to control its own distribution, or make it the supplier of choice for distributors. Large, established high-demand brands are less likely to be displaced by an emerging or new brand. Customers are unlikely to defect from a grocery store on the grounds that it did not carry a particular brand of toilet paper, but failure to carry Coca-Cola may well produce some defections.

Distribution, combined with A&P, is vital in attracting and retaining customers. The costs of running national television or magazine ads are invariant to brand size. For a small brand with lower margins, such costs consume a disproportionate share of total revenue. In addition, smaller brands typically have fewer distribution points compared to larger rivals, meaning higher costs per sale and fewer chances to connect with customers. There is a virtuous circle, giving larger players more bang for their buck.

USING A POWERFUL BRAND TO DRIVE GROWTH

Brand power can be enhanced through innovation and extensions. With creativity and advertising, strong existing brands can anchor expansion into new products and categories. Trends in fashion arise from the design innovation of style creators, but are stoked by a commercial payoff: change the color or shape of Oakley sunglasses and some people will discard their old pair and buy a new one to keep up with fashion. For a company like Luxottica, the ongoing practice turns something old-tech like sunglasses into an annuity stream.

Similarly, brands like Hermès or Louis Vuitton have gradually expanded from limited lines of ultra-expensive handbags and travel accessories to ready-to-wear clothing and sunglasses. Such innovation is less a function of big R&D budgets than the ability to exploit the full value of existing brands. Consider the feat of making the same product more expensive with a touch of branding finesse: put Swarovski crystals on a Moët & Chandon champagne bottle, package it as a premium gift, and it sells for multiples of the product's standard version.

Brands considered strong status symbols often offer significant innovation leadership – many luxury brands glide easily from handbag to perfumes or sunglasses. However, too many products can dilute the appeal. While companies like Louis Vuitton have limited expansion to a few related categories, there are examples of overreaching. Take Pierre Cardin. Initially a high-end fashion brand, the company licensed its brand out to products as diverse as cigarettes and pens. The end result has been a material dimming of the brand cachet.

Portfolio companies

While some large companies reap the bulk of revenue from a single brand – Hermès, Nike, Tiffany & Co. – many boast diverse portfolios of brands. Two of the best known examples of this are Procter & Gamble and Unilever. Distinguishing which among hundreds of brands are formidable as opposed to vulnerable is challenging. The challenge can be minimized by assessing product categories and seeking companies boasting branded products in more durable and economically attractive franchises. While not an ironclad rule, we believe that a portfolio of personal care products or luxury brands is generally superior to a portfolio of food brands.

A diversified brand portfolio offers several advantages. For one, when some products struggle, others absorb the loss and buy time to enable needed corrections. Additionally, brand diversity can contribute scale that pays off in more effective advertising and promotion, R&D and distribution. The combination of scale and brand diversity can also lead to attractive acquisition opportunities, especially to enable larger companies to buy smaller upstarts. The payoff is twofold, adding growth and combating competitors, which can be especially valuable in product lines where novelty matters to customers or where brand performance is volatile. The returns generated from acquiring promising, cutting-edge brands can also be enhanced by leveraging existing research, innovation, and distribution capabilities.

On the downside, managing a portfolio of brands requires a wider skill set than handling one or a few brands. Juggling many brands, especially in multiple segments, risks obscuring corporate focus and stretching management too thin. Resource stewardship must be ramped up to assure their most effective deployment across various lines.

LONGEVITY

One relatively simple way to assess brands is durability. The market can be a brutal evolutionary system. To survive for a long time in a competitive, sometimes cut-throat environment, a brand must have special qualities. Brands that have retained preferred status for decades have something special. While this doesn't insulate them entirely from future disruptions, such brands clearly have an enduring appeal that should help them to survive.

G. Innovation Dominance

Companies with high gross margins have more to invest in tactics to defend and grow their business, in areas such as R&D, A&P, or distribution. Such companies, able to invest more than their rivals, forge a virtuous cycle of growth: more spending drives revenues at high gross margins that spins off more investable resources. Spending on R&D – more specifically, on innovation – can be a particularly powerful part of this quality.

Innovation culture

Innovation dominance can facilitate both volume growth and pricing power. Even relatively simple developments in product design or unit size can be valuable. The same product offered in smaller packages can expand occasions of use (such as 'travel size') and potentially increase use by new or existing customers. Brand expansion into new categories can capture the benefits customers associate with the brand in new ways.

A culture of innovation dominance is attractive, particularly one that regularly renders new products. It is usually easier for companies to command higher prices and margins on new products versus old ones. When existing customers switch from the old to the new, the result tends to be a more attractive price mix. New products can also attract new customers, driving volume growth as well.

Innovation must be profitable to make innovation dominance attractive. Not all innovation makes a business better. In many industries, companies must innovate constantly simply to defend their position. When such innovation comes alongside declining margins (as R&D expenses are not covered by incremental sales), a company is engaged in costly cannibalization, not value creation.

To create value, innovation must increase volume or induce customer switching from a company's less-profitable to more-profitable offerings. In consumer goods, the most common way to achieve such switching is the trade-up to a more expensive version of an existing product. The path to 'premiumization' is often smoothest for products associated with social status or those conferring health advantages, where a higher price is often perceived to yield a greater benefit.

In markets where consumers are more cost conscious, or products are defined primarily by taste benefits, volume gains are often a better target for innovation. In our experience, products with clearly defined stand-alone taste benefits are harder to 'trade up' because of inculcation: consumers used to the taste of a certain cereal, soft drink or candy bar are unlikely to be persuaded of the merits of a new and improved version. Why, after all, is there no premium brand of Corn Flakes, Kit-Kat or Coca-Cola? Rather, for many food categories, innovation is focused on packaging or completely new flavors, both aimed at volume gains.

For corporate consumers, benefits from innovation need to be more tangible, such as appliances that slash energy costs. Since corporate buyers are often highly risk averse, incremental improvements are usually easier to sell than revolutionary innovations that require big changes to how the business operates or which create new, unknown risks.

Assuming customer appetite exists, the next question is how sustainable innovation can be. Difficulties may arise because advances have already been maximized – such as with basic calculators – or where there was a finite limit in the first place; there is only so much you can do with a cereal box.

The track record of category innovation can be a good guide to the future. Categories that have not made significant advances during the past five years are less likely to produce sustained and valuable innovation in the future than those that have made substantial progress during that time. In addition, superior prospects for innovation tend to occur in categories which have (at least perceived) significant scientific components, such as the personal care sector. Brands with records of successful innovation in a given category are likely to be capable of adaptive innovation in new categories – take, for example, Reckitt Benckiser's or Colgate's strong track records of innovating in apparently humdrum sectors from toothpaste and household cleaning products to cold remedies or foot care.

R&D-led innovation

Innovation dominance led by R&D is most common in companies commanding a large relative share of R&D spending in a given field. We aim to define these fields precisely in order to provide the most accurate assessment of relative share. If definitions are too broad, say the global pharmaceutical industry, hardly any company holds a large share. Narrowing this classification down, for example to oncology or diabetes care, enables a more meaningful assessment of which companies have a leading share of R&D spending.

While a dominant share of R&D spending doesn't guarantee predictable long-term outcomes, it can indicate a competitive edge. For example, Essilor's clear market leadership in the lens market is underpinned by the fact it accounts for around 75% of total industry R&D expenditure. Dominant companies also tend to enjoy a broader range of innovation opportunities. A business researching scores of alternate cosmetics formulas, for example, is more likely to find commercially prosperous combinations than one with a narrower research focus. The portfolio approach also increases the likelihood of maintaining innovation rates. When innovation stalls in one segment, others bear fruit.

Narrower product portfolios can lead to greater reliance on big breakthroughs. However, even where these big breakthroughs can be achieved, consumer response to them is notoriously unpredictable and so success is not guaranteed. Further, widespread anticipation of big breakthroughs often yields investor exuberance that suppresses investment returns.

Incremental innovation generally tends to produce more predictable revenue growth. Companies that have been able to improve customer benefits by a small increment annually for decades are more likely to keep doing so. By comparison, companies that have delivered a big breakthrough may or may not repeat this success. Moreover, incremental innovation tends to sit better with customers. Annual price increases of 5% for corresponding improvements become routine; abrupt price increases by a company with no track record of improvements provoke critical customer scrutiny about the price-value mix.

NOVO NORDISK: RESEARCH-LED INNOVATION

In the early 1920s, two Canadians, Dr. Frederick Banting and Professor John Macleod, succeeded in extracting and purifying a chemical from the pancreases of cattle: the feat earned them the 1923 Nobel Prize in Medicine. The pair had discovered insulin. Early results on diabetic patients were spectacular and insulin remains the primary treatment for diabetes. Today, half the global insulin market is served by a single company, Denmark's Novo Nordisk.

Novo Nordisk is the product of a 1989 merger that reunited those two entities after a split that occurred generations earlier. Nordisk Insulin Laboratorium was founded in Copenhagen, Denmark, in the mid-1920s. After an internal disagreement, the company's primary engineer, Harald Pedersen, and his brother left the business and started a competitor, Novo Terapeutisk Laboratorium.

With Nordisk dominating in Scandinavia, Novo focused overseas. Both companies grew significantly and at the time of the reunification, which brought an end to over 60 years of competition, they were the second and third ranked players in the diabetes space, behind Eli Lilly. Diabetes treatment now accounts for around three-quarters of Novo Nordisk's profit.

The incidence of diabetes globally has increased rapidly in the last decade, driven by the global pandemic of obesity – now numbering more than 600 million people and forecast to continue rising. Demand for diabetes treatment will, we believe, increase more rapidly due to rising diagnosis rates; as will the continued need for better treatments and broader reach of care (fewer than 10% of afflicted people receive effective care).

Novo Nordisk has benefited from these trends, growing organic revenue growth at a 12% compound annual growth rate over the past decade along with a 19% growth rate in earnings. These are tailwinds, however, because the real deep value behind the company is its sustained and successful commitment to R&D, which is part of its corporate culture.

Historically, the company has led numerous industry breakthroughs, such as converting porcine into human insulin in 1982 and introducing a pen to facilitate self-dosing in 1985, and now boasts a full portfolio of modern insulin products, spanning the fast-acting (prandial), basal and pre-mix categories. Recent research focuses both on improving dosing of existing treatments as well as striving for new ones. Pipeline products are abundant, including new rollouts of more effective products with faster action or more extended duration.

Novo spent nearly $2 billion on R&D in 2014, six times its level of 20 years earlier, reflecting its sustained investment in research in proportion to its size. The long-term dedication to research reflects that a majority of the company's voting shares are held by the Novo Nordisk Foundation, a research force that also backs Chr. Hansen.

The value of Novo's relentless innovation is maximized through highly efficient manufacturing capacity, which benefits from economies of scale, and a significant global sales footprint, which enables reaching its large and fragmented target audience. Such competitive advantages have driven stand-out returns on capital exceeding 70%. Combined with operating margins set to exceed 40% in 2015 and its strong, stable growth track record, these metrics are peerless among large European corporations.

H. Forward Integrators

Under the right conditions, forward integration can be hugely valuable. There are several types of forward integration, including store ownership, franchising, licensing and internet selling (e-tailing), each of which we examine below. Typically, the most successful forward integrators are powerful global brands: weaker brands struggle to draw shoppers to stores or traffic to websites. Consider LVMH's own-store expansion over the past decade, Nike's success online (sales already exceed $1 billion), or the continued growth of franchised hotel brands such as Marriott or Holiday Inn. Whichever route is taken, the payoff can be great, though there are costs to consider in the form of incremental capital requirements and added complexity.

Strategic value

Forward integration gives companies more influence over customer experiences. Consumers respond not just to products, but to brand image and even to advice and guidance. In retail stores, clever merchandising can stimulate customers to trade up and explore new things, as they try on clothes or smell perfume. Companies which control the store-front are able to shape these buying experiences more precisely. Above all, producers who sell direct name their own prices, instead of ceding control to warehouses, distributors or retailers. What's more, they exercise a mini-monopoly in their own stores, without competing brands or private labels vying for space.

Offense and defense

Forward integration can strengthen a company's position versus competitors. For some companies, selling and promoting products in the right location cements a company's brand and reputation, whether on Fifth Avenue in New York, Bond Street in London or Rodeo Drive in Los Angeles. With a shortage of such locations available, it can take years for newer brands to build the kind of store-front offering needed to give a brand the desired cachet.

Forward integration can also ease entry into new markets. Companies that control their own stores and infrastructure depend less on the kindness of strangers to promote the company's benefits. Dependence on partners or other companies in supply chains can prove particularly tricky in emerging markets, where verifying reliability can be difficult. In our view, companies that take the time to build their own operations from scratch are more likely to succeed than those who are at the mercy of third parties.

Forward integration can help a company to build scale among stakeholders that it could not otherwise reach. For example, the world's leading sunglass manufacturer, Luxottica, has a substantially stronger bargaining position with other brands thanks to its ownership of the Sunglass Hut retail chain.

Franchising

The economics of a strong franchise model are often compelling. In its purest form, a franchise-based business provides growth funded by third parties – franchisees – and theoretically infinite returns on capital. Franchising is arguably the ultimate expression of brand power: franchisees pay fees for the right to use a brand. The fee level is justified by the economic power of the brand.

Take Holiday Inn, a brand owned and franchised by InterContinental Hotels Group. Franchisees pay approximately 5% of revenues, through good times and bad, for the right to put the Holiday Inn flag above their hotel door. The franchisees, in turn, gain access to the branded firm's well-established central booking system, which drives the majority of sales. The result for the business is a higher level of revenue per available room, an industry benchmark, relative to rivals.

Since revenues are more stable over time than net income, the revenue-based franchise fee adds predictability to the franchisor's return. For the franchisor, expansion requires modest incremental capital, as franchisees are typically responsible for providing most of the assets, including property, fixtures and fittings. Franchisor margins are also high: InterContinental Hotels Group boasts EBIT margins exceeding 80% in its franchise division. Once critical mass is established, the incremental profit contribution from additional franchised revenue is substantial.

Successful franchising models generally have two characteristics. First, the underlying business needs powerful economics: strong enough for a third party to make an attractive return even after paying a fee to the brand owner. Second, there is a minimum scale requirement: the company must have the infrastructure to support a franchise system and the financial firepower to support a brand with A&P.

Such characteristics are developed over time. Most predominantly-franchised businesses have gradually migrated from making money and building brand equity in company-owned outlets. It is difficult to franchise out a new, unestablished brand. However, where the right conditions exist, the benefits can be material for both the franchisee and the brand owner.

PHYSICAL AND ONLINE PRESENCE

It may seem obvious that commercial enterprises must have an online presence today, but the success of this type of forward integration is not guaranteed. A good starting point is a powerful global brand. The success of the Nike and (Inditex's) Zara online businesses underlines how compelling such a strategy can be for brands that already enjoy a strong position in the consumers' consciousness. A second important factor is logistics infrastructure and capabilities. A direct-to-consumer online offering can add material complexities (and costs). Those businesses able to leverage existing infrastructure are often best positioned to succeed: Nike and Inditex being exemplars once again.

Forward integration via online retailing can also dovetail well with physical forward integration, suggested by examples as varied as Apple Stores and Nestlé's Nespresso outlets. These company-owned stores, one purveying iPads, the other coffee, both launched in the early 2000s as the move to online retailing was gathering momentum. Both used physical stores to enhance customer experiences by picking good locations (exclusive locations help confer status) and emphasizing service and advice (the Genius bar in Apple Stores and free coffees at Nespresso). Coupled with a strong online offering, the retail outlets helped both companies to develop a powerful ecosystem that allowed them closer control of customer experiences and which delivered higher margins by cutting out middlemen.

LUXOTTICA: FORWARD INTEGRATOR

Luxottica, founded in 1961 as a small manufacturer of components for the Italian optical industry, may not be a household name, but in the market for premium eyeglasses and sunglasses it is everywhere. Luxottica's stable of brands is iconic, encompassing Oakley and Ray-Ban, and it boasts a starry licensed portfolio featuring Armani, Bulgari, Burberry, Chanel, Polo Ralph Lauren, and Prada. In recent decades, the company has expanded through a series of brave but astute deals to become its sector's decisive global leader.

Luxottica exemplifies successful forward integration, starting decades ago with manufacturing and today spanning the value chain through to the end consumer. Luxottica's forward integration started in the 1970s when it added wholesale distribution to its manufacturing capabilities. Initially focused in Italy, this strategy expanded internationally in the 1980s. The shift allowed the company to leverage its manufacturing prowess more effectively and profitably through increased control of customer relationships.

The company took the logical next step in 1995 when it acquired the business that owned LensCrafters, a leading North American optical retailer, becoming the first leading eyewear manufacturer to add retailing capabilities. Following the success of this strategic move, Luxottica hugely expanded its retail program across formats and markets, and it now owns GMO, OPSM, Pearle Vision (North America), and Sunglass Hut among others.

Luxottica's forward integration increases profitability, since less value from design, manufacturing and brand ownership leaks away through the chain. It lets the company build brand awareness and dictate trends, significantly reducing the risk of a fashion 'miss', since Luxottica is an arbiter of what is in vogue. Owning retail stores guarantees product distribution, a benefit that extends to specifics such as shelf location, in-store marketing and knowledgeable sales reps. Owners of the licensed brands cite distribution capability as one of the main reasons that they are drawn to Luxottica. Retail ownership also affords better consumer insight than a manufacturer possesses, meaning better design decisions.

The company's strength across the value chain positions it for dominance. Its platform facilitates superior acquisition synergies compared to rivals, regardless of deal type. For example, a newly acquired brand can be distributed through the world's most comprehensive network of more than 7,000 stores of its own and more than 150,000 other outlets in 130 countries (a benefit that also applies to newly licensed bands). After acquiring a retailer, Luxottica can immediately push an unparalleled product portfolio through the store base – true for physical chains as well as online merchandisers. This unmatched prowess means that stand-alone companies are worth vastly more once incorporated into the Luxottica family.

Forward integration into retail does not always confer such significant benefits on manufacturers. It tends to increase the fixed cost base, impairing needed flexibility for companies in volatile industries or with weak brands where demand fluctuates. But the eyewear industry is relatively stable and Luxottica combines sophisticated manufacturing and logistics with a powerful brand portfolio. Can you imagine a premium sunglasses shop *not* stocking Oakley or Ray-Ban?

Luxottica's unique position has led to strong, steady organic sales growth and sustainably high returns on capital, along with plentiful cash generation to fund continuing tuck-in acquisitions.

I. Market Share Gainers

A basic measure of company quality is propensity to gain market share. A company with better products (in terms of quality and/or price) and superior execution should regularly attract new customers from competitors and widen its reach among existing consumers.

The power of market share

Market share gains drive growth. By drawing customers from rivals, such growth can be isolated from overall market growth and hence less dependent on macroeconomic variables.

Market share gains reinforce competitive advantages based on scale. The largest companies among competitors command larger budgets for everything from R&D to advertising. Distributors consider them more important than smaller firms and especially value those whose market is growing.

A subtler and broader halo effect adds value: most stakeholders – including suppliers, distributors and employees – prefer to play on the winning team. They are likely to be diligent to retain their top spot.

A rule with exceptions

There are several exceptions to the rule of preferring consistent gains in market share, particularly short term. A company facing rapid increases in costs may wisely choose to raise prices ahead of competitors, at the expense of market share. In such cases, letting market share slide may be a rational decision.

Similarly, except for companies committed to being the low-cost producer, we are wary of sacrificing price and gross margins for the sake of market share. Such behavior raises questions about a brand's actual benefit to customers. If price is enough to drive share up and down then customers clearly place great emphasis on price rather than other product benefits.

In industries where growth and economics can be detached for significant periods of time, short-term market share gains may be a negative. Take industries such as insurance and bank lending. Gaining market share in bank lending is easy: simply lower credit standards. The risk from such behavior may not appear for years when defaults occur, as the credit default swaps at the heart of the 2008 financial crisis highlighted. Likewise, insurance companies can quickly gain share by relaxing underwriting discipline, with associated losses delayed until claims are filed. In these settings, market share must be viewed with a correspondingly long horizon. While quality companies should still gain share over the long run, in these industries they likely cede share during economic booms and gain during economic busts.

FIELMANN: MARKET SHARE GAINER

For nearly half the developed world's population, the first task of every morning – even before checking email – is to reach for the device that allows them to see: glasses. Spectacles have morphed from medical necessity into fashion accessory, with the latest styles advertised by glamorous celebrities. This was not always the case.

As recently as the 1980s, health insurance plans offered vision coverage limited to a small set of dull, monochrome, and unfashionable frames. The vision-impaired who wanted something more had to pay and costs were high, leaving many to suffer the stigma associated with cheap eyewear. Manufacturers accepted the status quo, which allowed them to charge a premium price for fancy glasses, while opticians enjoyed a comfortable living from fitting a few pairs a day.

In Germany, one man drove change: Guenther Fielmann, who opened his first optician store in 1972. From the outset, he pursued a strategy of selling fancier glasses at lower prices, forgoing some of the high potential margin per unit to drive volume growth. His more fashionable, yet thrifty, frames proved an attractive proposition to price-conscious Germans.

Fielmann proceeded to build a chain of stores. As volume increased, he improved his purchasing terms by cutting out the wholesaler. But Fielmann's major breakthrough came in 1981, when he struck a deal with the German state health insurer to let him offer 90 new, more fashionable, frames to customers at the same insurance cost as the existing few standard-issue frames.

This was a masterstroke, as suddenly huge numbers of customers could enjoy a wide variety of fashionable glasses with third-party payment. Volume growth spiked. Fielmann leveraged the growth to backward integrate, sourcing its own-label frames and lenses, and optimizing the entire retail process. Pricing cuts, savvy marketing, and retail integration forged Fielmann's path to market dominance. Today, Fielmann's share of the German eyewear market exceeds 50%, yet it sells this volume through stores representing only 5% of the store base.

With scale and integration come cost advantages. Fielmann's unit cost is an estimated quarter of its rivals. Given that its volume moves through such a small portion of the market's total store base, Fielmann's relative fixed costs are also comparatively low. To encapsulate, Fielmann sells 20 times more glasses per day per store than its rivals at a much lower unit cost with fractional overheads. Even with lower prices, therefore, we estimate that Fielmann nets as much per pair of glasses as rivals but at higher margins, approaching 20%.

Fielmann's fortress-like market position is reinforced by yet another advantage: leadership in the labor market. A substantial barrier to industry growth is lack of qualified staff, as the unemployment rate for German opticians is barely above 1%. One reason is German law, which requires that optical shops be run by master opticians; a status that takes three or more years to attain. While rivals struggle, Fielmann runs an optician training academy and trains 3,000 eye care professionals annually, amounting to nearly 40% of industry apprentices.

The German optical industry may not sound like the hottest growth market – and it isn't. But the qualities that enabled Fielmann to take market share at a rate of 1-2% annually for a few decades are compelling. The share gains drive attractive long-term compound earnings growth (EPS has tripled in the past decade). With limited capital requirements for growth, cash is ample, despite a dividend payout ratio of 85%. Nor is there any sign of the company's cost or price advantages eroding. Indeed, given Fielmann's influence over the labor pool, prospects for future market share gain remain as strong as ever.

J. GLOBAL CAPABILITIES AND LEADERSHIP

History is littered with examples of impressive domestic franchises that were eroded by the encroachment of foreign rivals. In the 1980s, European consumer electronics makers all but disappeared after Japanese manufacturers entered the market with higher quality and better priced alternatives. In the 1990s, England's financial industry, a cozy coterie of large firms centered in London, was shocked to find American investment banks aggressively muscling in on their territory.

Other strong domestic companies try to project their might abroad only to fail, proving unable to transplant their strengths. A recent example is provided by Tesco, the venerable British grocer whose efforts to expand globally backfired.

We seek out those companies that prove able to project strength outward, entering and conquering foreign markets. The pattern they fit is having demonstrable global capabilities, often backed by industry leadership. Successful global expansion tends to reflect a number of factors, prominently including experience, product differentiation and adaptability.

By *global industry leadership*, we are referring more to product differentiation and business model than scale. A global industry leader's business model and products must stack up well against competitors in other markets. For example, Rolls-Royce engines compete well against any jet engine from US peers Pratt & Whitney or General Electric. While Rolls-Royce will not win every battle, it always has a good shot.

A focus on global leadership is warranted for two reasons. For one, it is unsafe to assume that even the most powerful domestic company will remain dominant when there are superior peers operating in the same industry abroad. While these potential competitors may never choose to enter the domestic market in question, their very existence presents a large unquantifiable risk that is best avoided. Even companies with localized advantages such as scale in retailing can be affected, which is evident from the disruption of grocery markets from Spain to the UK by the German deep-discounters.

The other reason to stress global leadership relates to ability to expand. Without industry leadership, companies struggle to enter new markets. Offering products that can win customers as easily in Boston as in Beijing is therefore a big plus.

A good indication that a company has global capabilities is a track record of successfully adapting a business model from one setting to another, at home and abroad. Many European companies started in small countries, so they were often forced to develop the ability to expand into new markets: witness the expansion of Swedish engineering firms such as ASSA ABLOY and Atlas Copco. Larger European companies like Shell, Nestlé, and Unilever honed their global capabilities decades ago when large parts of the world were still under European influence. We view such experience positively; it opens the door for more sustainable growth than geographically constrained companies can manage.

Willingness and ability to adapt to local tastes, cultures, and logistical challenges is critical. A great example is Yum!, which owns the KFC and Pizza Hut brands. A quick glance at a KFC or Pizza Hut menu in Beijing would be enough to show how much these brands have adapted to cater to local tastes. In addition to the chicken and pizza that US patrons would recognize, the restaurants meet local demand for a variety of traditional Chinese food from rice dishes and spicy soups to congee. Such adaptability is often the result of considerable trial and error and takes time – both brands have been in China since the 1990s. The effort yields significant payoffs, including making Yum! the largest restaurant operator in China, boasting some 5,000 KFC outlets and 1,700 Pizza Huts.

INDITEX: GLOBAL CAPABILITIES

Amancio Ortega Gaona opened the first Zara store in A Coruña, Spain in 1975, purveying the latest fashions at affordable prices. The strategy remains unchanged to this day. The difference now is that the parent company, Inditex, is one of a handful of truly global fashion retailers. The company's sheer scale is enviable: in 2014, it generated $20 billion of sales from 6,683 stores across the world, distributing more than one billion garments. The founder still owns nearly 60% of the company and is, according to the Bloomberg Billionaires list, the second richest man in the world.

The company's first store outside Spain opened in Portugal in 1988, heralding a sustained global push. Zara, generating two-thirds of group sales, has been the heart of expansion, but Inditex has successfully launched seven other concepts, including the more upmarket Massimo Dutti and the edgier youth brand Bershka. Today, the company operates in 88 countries and generates 81% of sales outside Spain. As a touchstone, H&M and Gap operate from approximately half the number of stores in about 55 markets.

Inditex is a beneficiary of the globalization of fashion. However, its explosive international expansion and consistent outperformance of its peers reflects a unique 'demand pull' model and the tight control of all stages of the fashion value chain from design through sale. Most of its retail peers take fashion risks by ordering collections as much as one year in advance. Inditex, in contrast, orders less than half its garments ahead of season, affording store managers flexibility to top up offerings continuously as demand indicates. Store sales are analyzed daily using advanced algorithms to suggest optimal inventory composition for each store.

Deliveries are received biweekly in small batches, ensuring that only the best-selling items are displayed in store. This system allows Inditex to avoid major fashion misses and to adjust quickly to local vagaries in weather. Collections share characteristics across borders, with few minor adjustments (such as slightly smaller tailored suits for men in the Far East). Critical to its global success, the demand pull model allows the company to quickly adapt its offering to reflect local preferences across its international markets.

Whereas many peers still source predominantly from the Far East, Inditex sources nearly two-thirds of stock from regions close to its main distribution centers in Spain (such as Morocco), contributing to its market-leading average four-week lead times from design to store. In-house design teams continuously fine-tune top sellers and create new garments, more than 80% produced in response to data collected from the stores. The company's full price sales rate exceeds 80%, well above the industry average of about 65%.

Distribution is also rapid. Most items are delivered straight to stores from the main distribution center in Spain. Outside Europe, this is mainly achieved by air to maximize speed. Underpinning this is a continual investment in technology, epitomized by automated distribution centers and globally standardized information technology. Additionally, store managers, whose bonus compensation exceeds market rates, have deep knowledge of local markets, driving high sales densities.

The premium store locations, with constantly changing displays, are the company's main form of advertising. The combination of high gross profits per store, negligible requirement to invest in hefty local infrastructure and a business model that does not rely on advertising makes it easier for Inditex to enter new markets. All stores are expected to be profitable on a stand-alone basis, from the sole Pull & Bear store in Panama to the flagship Zara store in New York.

Inditex's unique fast-fashion operating model produces high gross margins. Since 2000, the company has generated compounded annual growth in sales of 15% and pre-tax income of 17%, with same store sales growth averaging 5% annually and positive in all these years. Despite its vast scale, the highly fragmented nature of the apparel industry means that the company's market share is still less than 1% in most countries. The runway for further expansion remains considerable.

K. Corporate Culture

Quality companies tend to have a strong sense of culture based on a core set of common values that drive success. These values vary by company, but examples include cost consciousness for a low-cost provider, scientific curiosity for a research-driven company, and team spirit in collaborative production businesses such as providing third-party certifications of credit quality or financial reporting.

In probing culture, we consult management, of course, but we equally value input from other corporate constituents. Suppliers or customers can describe execution experiences that reflect on a company's priorities, norms and values. Former employees can reveal hidden traits worth uncovering. While they and others may have their own agendas in discussing corporate culture, collecting a large number of perspectives typically facilitates a reliable snapshot.

Trustworthiness

Trustworthiness is common among quality companies. We view investing as a long-term relationship, the essence of which is trust. Trust is predicated on honesty and integrity. As with other investors, we avoid staking funds in dishonest or dishonourable organizations, and fortunately thoroughly crooked corporate cultures are rare. But in business, some people and companies are more trustworthy than others. The difference often manifests itself in small revelations of corporate culture.

A common example concerns handling of bad news. Some companies obfuscate or delay reporting adverse developments while others promptly and forthrightly disclose them. While often dismissed as a matter of corporate communication or legal requirement, the difference reflects profoundly on relative trustworthiness. A corporate culture of open and frank confrontation of facts is healthy. The approach to sharing information externally is also likely to be mirrored internally: managers who mislead the market are likely training employees to mislead them. Likewise, we value companies that voluntarily confide their mistakes and discuss the lessons learned from them, because such exercises reflect a corporate culture committed to experimentation and improvement.

Long term

Running a business is a long-term affair. Products take years to develop; winning the trust of customers and building scale in new markets can take even longer. We look for corporate cultures that manifest a long-term vision and companies that share our quest for long-term value creation. Such companies understand the importance of cost efficiency but focus on long-term sustainable growth and return on capital.

Short-term earnings goals are readily achieved by cost cutting, and revenue growth targets can be hit through an aggressive acquisition campaign. We prefer companies which play the long game by allocating capital to organic capex, R&D and advertising in order to drive long-term growth. Even though media and analysts fixate on quarterly earnings per share, we prize companies that prioritize return on capital. In general, we also like companies that use return on capital to measure performance and influence incentive compensation plans not only for top management, but throughout the organization. This tends to indicate a more considered and long-term culture than companies where compensation is linked solely to earnings growth.

Execution

The ability to deliver on time and according to plan is highly valuable. Timely execution is usually embedded in corporate culture.

If it is not, when deadlines loom or backlogs grow, workers wonder why they should stay late or work overtime when others leave early or stay home. We look for firms where diligence is stimulated and rewarded, where people are eager to go the extra mile.

A few telltale signs indicate an ability to execute. For example, companies that are good at executing tend to be less 'accident'-prone. They do not suddenly announce big cost overruns on their latest information technology or recently discovered kinks in an acquisition made two years earlier. They are organizations that tend to deliver on their promises, small as well as large. That doesn't mean everything always goes to plan, just that mishaps occur more rarely. More importantly, when things do go wrong, they are usually able to identify the problem and fix it with dispatch.

Companies that execute well also tend to be knowledgeable about their market. Ask these companies detailed questions about what is going on in a certain market or region and they know the answer. This is a beneficial side effect of making execution a high priority. The result is often a pattern of steady small adjustments made routinely – updating systems or shifting to offshore locations – rather than bold reorganizations and grand master plans.

Self-perpetuation

Industries and companies tend to recruit people with personalities that fit the associated culture. Creative types are an asset for the design of haute couture, but are not the ideal choice to help build nuclear reactors. Similarly, a deep-rooted cost culture is more critical to a low-cost provider than for purveyors of premium brands. Cultures, as a result, tend to self-perpetuate.

Companies with questionable practices are more in danger of attracting people unwilling to raise ethical issues or report wrongdoing. People prone to bending the rules are likely to survive and even prosper in organizations that tolerate deviance.

Family ownership

Many companies we have owned over the past decade have large inter-generational family ownership. This reflects the parallels between what we look for and what such family businesses offer: a focus on long-term value creation. In addition, durable dynastic firms typically avoid excessive leverage and use retained earnings rather than serial equity offerings to grow.[31] Family-owned businesses can of course fail, sometimes through misplaced confidence in the abilities of second or third generation managers. Here the distinction between family-owned and family-run can be important – research tends to confirm our hunch that corporate cultures of family-owned businesses often align them with the criteria of quality investing.

A McKinsey study of global organizational health found that family-owned firms have particularly good corporate cultures, along with high levels of worker motivation and strong leadership.[32] Another study by researchers at IE Business School in Madrid found that family-controlled firms in Europe regularly outperform peers in market valuation, revenue growth, and returns on assets.[33] Notably, results span geographies and industries, indicating something peculiar about family-owned companies rather than regions or sectors.

SVENSKA HANDELSBANKEN: CORPORATE CULTURE

While banks worldwide sank amid the global financial crisis of 2008, Svenska Handelsbanken of Sweden excelled. Fundamental structures and attitudes – the stuff of corporate culture – explain why.

The bank, founded in the 1870s, took its current cultural shape in the 1970s under the leadership of CEO Jan Wallander. Handelsbanken's motto – "the branch is the bank" – reflects its thoroughly decentralized structure. Branch managers make all operating decisions for their branch, on location: hiring; product offerings; and client outreach and management. Each branch manager is accordingly fully responsible for their branch's profit and loss, with no deflecting of responsibility to other departments or functions.

One result of such local knowledge and clear responsibility is Handelsbanken's superior credit loss performance. Another is how the bank consistently scores at the top of customer satisfaction surveys. These practices also explain why Handelsbanken is successfully bucking adverse banking industry trends: as rivals close branches and centralize customer relations, Handelsbanken is doing the opposite.

While other banks pay bankers bonuses that skew incentives toward high-risk strategies, Handelsbanken pays no bonuses for top executives or risk-takers. Rather, Handelsbanken offers a profit-sharing system for all employees, much of which is invested in Handelsbanken shares. One result: employees are the bank's largest shareholders. Such a structure breeds loyalty: staff turnover is far below the industry average.

Risk aversion is deeply embedded in Handelsbanken culture. Its management philosophy is to take risks only in areas where it has demonstrable strengths and to minimize all others. It has consistently run a conservative liquidity profile, with superlative capital ratios and longer duration of funding versus peers. Unlike most large European banks, Handelsbanken eschews high-risk, speculative proprietary trading.

These cultural traits explain why, during the global financial crisis of 2008, Handelsbanken was a net lender to peer banks and the overall banking system, including lending to the Swedish Central Bank. In an earlier financial crisis afflicting Swedish banks in the early 1990s, Handelsbanken was also the beacon of strength: it was the only Swedish bank that did not receive state aid or become nationalized.

Such risk aversion is also evident in how the company approaches growth. The expansion of most European banks has typically been by acquisitions or speculative capital allocation into Eastern Europe and emerging markets, with little success. Handelsbanken's model allows it to pursue profitable organic growth in safer and more stable markets, such as the Nordic states and, more recently, the UK.

Financial returns reflect these distinctive structures and attitudes: steady organic earnings growth combined with regular market share gains have translated into Handelsbanken outperforming its Nordic peer group in return on equity every single year for the last 43 years.

Since late 2007, returns to owners (increases in equity plus dividends) have compounded at 15%. While the vast majority of European banks earn less today than before the crisis and their average share prices have halved, Handelsbanken earns more and its share price has more than doubled. Culture pays.

L. COST TO REPLICATE

One way of assessing the durability of a competitive advantage is to invert the analysis. Instead of looking at what supports a competitive advantage, we analyze what it would take for a newcomer to replicate the business and remove the advantage. Such analysis often reveals idiosyncrasies that can be instructive in assessing a business's quality.

Take two examples. In the liquor business, white spirits are probably more at risk from disruption than brown spirits, no matter how strong the brand. While clever marketing and deep pockets enable new entrants to develop a competitive brand of gin or vodka, it is challenging to do with cognac or whiskeys. For one, brown spirits require aging, entailing not merely creativity and resources but unusual patience (often over ten years) for rivals to have even a shot at building a credible portfolio of brands. At the other end of the spectrum, in the white spirit market, potatoes can be transformed into cash within the space of a month.

Or consider backward induction in aircraft engine manufacturing. While capital is rarely an insuperable barrier to entry, the engine industry has spent billions in the past decade on R&D. All of that investment has generated proprietary technology that would be difficult to match. In addition, the industry generates substantial revenues from servicing engines apart from selling them, giving them a long time horizon over which to recoup investment. Start-ups in this field would also have to overcome the considerable attachment that manufacturers like Airbus and Boeing have to their stalwart suppliers.

EXPERIAN: THE FORBIDDING COSTS OF REPLICATION

The United Kingdom's credit reporting industry dates to 1803, when a group of London tailors started sharing information about deadbeat customers. In 1826, the wonderfully named 'Society of Guardians for the Protection of Tradesmen against Swindlers, Sharpers and other Fraudulent Persons' was established in Manchester. Later that century, several credit agencies were founded in the United States, including Jim Chilton's Merchants Credit Association, which provided annual printed credit directories to subscribers and pioneered two enduring initiatives: collecting positive as well as negative information and convincing member merchants to confidentially share credit information for associational use.

Chilton's business and the Manchester society would, many years later, become part of Experian, a global leader in today's credit information business. Experian's primary asset is a massive database of consumer credit data contributed over many decades by legions of financial institutions, retailers, utilities, and other creditors. To enrich the database, the company harvests extensive information from numerous public sources and exclusive data sets. Data has been accumulated and synthesized through outlets worldwide, from the UK and the US to Brazil.

In the UK, the foundation was Britain's largest retailer and consumer creditor, Great Universal Stores (GUS). It computerized its data in the 1960s and added vast information from electoral rolls and court records, and began commercializing the product in 1980. In 1996, GUS acquired the leading US credit rating agency, owned by TRW, whose founders include Dr. Si Ramo, the rocket scientist. Among Ramo's prescient prophecies (besides his 1961 vision of a cashless society) were automating credit reporting, predicting payment patterns, and scoring credit quality. Ramo and TRW spent decades vindicating those prophesies, as they collected and standardized volumes of consumer credit information. In 2007, Experian (as the combined UK and US business was then known) acquired Serasa, Brazil's market leader in the field, founded in 1968 by a consortium of regional banks.

Through such global agglomerations of venerable data compilers, Experian's databases are the product of a lengthy and intense process of collecting, matching, contrasting, verifying, and analyzing abundant information. Contemporary global systems add incremental bits of information daily, each being trivial but when added to the storehouse able to enhance credit histories and facilitate pattern recognition. So besides costing a fortune to build, data accumulate daily that amplify returns. Individual data contributors expect to benefit from the aggregation of credit information from fellow creditors, creating a powerful network effect.

The result is an industry prone to consolidation. In the US, the market is dominated by three credit agencies with approximately even market shares; outside the US, most markets are duopolies, with one dominant and one subservient rival. Barriers to entry are formidable from scale, complexity and pricing. Experian also leverages its core assets into related areas, such as data analytics. Both its core and complementary businesses involve products – information – that can be sold multiple times, slashing marginal costs.

Outcomes are impressive: solid ten-year organic sales CAGR of 6% for the group and growing operating margins from 21% a decade ago to 27% today. The foundation of these strong results is the company's unique and irreplaceable database assets.

* * *

Financial theory assumes that abnormal performance is unsustainable and that outsized growth, profits, margins or returns are destined to return to the average. The patterns identified show how some companies can overcome the forces of mean reversion over long periods of time. Correctly analyzing these patterns is not always easy and, in the next chapter, we discuss some pitfalls to avoid in the hunt for quality companies.

CHAPTER THREE
PITFALLS

ATTERNS OF QUALITY ARE NOT THE ONLY routes to achieving the attractive economic characteristics of cash generation, high returns on capital, and growth. Indeed, some companies that achieve such results are exposed to unstable or transient factors that jeopardize long-term sustainability.

Companies that are prosperous today may depend on forces that are susceptible to unpredictable but rapid change. Many appear stronger than they are due to cyclical growth, the temporary tailwinds of fickle consumer trends, or technological leadership vulnerable to disruption. While such forces are too nuanced to automatically rule out consideration of companies exposed to them, they warrant greater scrutiny because of the significant downside risks.

In this chapter, we explore the subtleties of cyclicality first, followed by the hazards of technology, dependency, and shifting customer preferences.

A. Cyclicality

Cyclicality is a fact of business life. The economic fortunes of a company's end markets ebb and flow, often in unpredictable ways. For a fortunate few, fluctuations are small enough that they barely register, but for many, vicissitudes are tidal. Significant cyclicality can mask problems as well as disrupt or even thwart value creation.

Prudence dictates minimizing exposure to deeply cyclical industries, such as energy and mining, where many companies sell commoditized products. Such companies rarely command sustainable competitive advantages. However, cycles also recur among purveyors of branded and other differentiated products boasting competitive advantages. Even quality companies must battle this reality and investors are better off confronting the fact head on.

Cyclicality complicates the operating environment, taking control of important levers of value creation like pricing and mix optimization, costs, and capital expenditure. Expansionary periods may induce overinvestment, which leaves inadequate capital for investment in ensuing downturns. Pronounced cyclicality can encourage short-term thinking.

This section opens with an examination of the risks associated with extreme supply-demand cyclicality then, via a discussion of the benefits of *flow products*, moves on to look at the challenges created by a cyclical customer base and the difficulties of analysing extended cycles.

We should underline that cyclicality per se is not something we seek to avoid. As we discuss at the end of this section, many quality companies in cyclical industries are able to use these vicissitudes to their advantage, investing counter-cyclically and using periods of disruption to widen their lead. Several of our most successful long-term investments are companies exposed to clear industrial and consumer cycles, which have been able to use their sustainable competitive advantage to grow through-cycle.

SUPPLY-DEMAND CYCLICALITY

The least attractive form of cyclicality effect occurs in pure supply-demand industries, such as steel making or offshore drilling. In these industries, products tend to be uniform and significant capital outlays are necessary for production.

During expansionary cycles, capacity additions are stimulated by high demand. A snapshot at that moment would reflect a robust and profitable industry. Expansions can last so long that most participants and many observers begin to believe that a structural change has occurred to eliminate the cycle. The economic expansion of the early 2000s led to such beliefs becoming prevalent in the years leading up to the great contraction of 2008.

When the economy shifts, as it inevitably does, demand drops and the costs of over-capacity come due. As demand drops, prices fall and profits suffer. In such an environment, it is virtually impossible to plot the future price path, to forecast its low-point or predict the duration of the downturn. In theory, economists' marginal cost curves should illuminate the break points where participants will stop producing and stability will return. In practice, however, producers do not conform to economic models, as managers pursue agendas to maintain production despite the directives of marginal cost theory.

In supply-demand industries, some companies may command competitive advantages by being low-cost producers. But the economic value of such a trait is hard to assess when prices are next to impossible to predict. An oil company that can extract oil at a cost of $20 per barrel may have a cost competitive advantage. However, determining the value of the cash flow of such an advantage depends entirely on whether the long-term oil price is $40 or $100 per barrel.

THE QUIET APPEAL OF FLOW PRODUCTS

Many companies have customers facing cyclicality in end-markets, meaning that demand for their own products fluctuates, but not necessarily price levels. Examples appear among suppliers of equipment or services to industries such as paper, mining, oil and gas, or agriculture. To exclude investing in all such companies would be unwise. In fact, nearly all companies selling to the industrial sector face the problem to varying degrees, including quality businesses such as Atlas Copco and ASSA ABLOY. Rather, we focus on whether the company's economic model depends on the customer's capital expenditure or operating costs.

A business that is solely linked to customers' capital expenditure makes for a much more complicated investment than one linked to their operating costs. In most cyclical industries, capital equipment is purchased amid periods of capacity expansion. When iron ore prices rise, mining companies plan and build new mines; but when they fall, new projects are postponed or cancelled.

For a company whose profits are dependent on such capital expenditure, it is extremely difficult to predict results. Even a rough guess requires insight into both commodity pricing and how miners evaluate investing in new capacity at different price levels. A more reliable estimate would consider long-term demand trends for the given commodity. While some industrial economists with related expertise might be able to model this, we find it too challenging to translate into a predictable cash flow pattern and therefore tend to steer clear.

On the other hand, for a company whose profits tie to customers' operating costs, cyclicality poses less risk of disruption and remains relatively predictable. Even during cyclical downturns when prices are low, most producers maintain existing facilities and even production levels while cutting capital expenditures. When oil prices fall, producers still produce. So long as production is substantially maintained, suppliers of products tied to production and operating costs typically face less disruption from the cycle.

We call these *flow products*. Mills have to be maintained. Production equipment requires spare parts and regular maintenance.

Tests must be run on extracted oil or minerals. So companies with most of their profit pools from flow products tend to experience less profit erosion during downturns. Likewise, during upturns, theirs are not among the products that spike in demand, aiding prediction. In both phases of the cycle, this is especially true for differentiated rather than commoditized products. Therefore, we like to focus on flow products with genuine differentiation benefits.

The relative attractiveness of flow products versus capex products offers two broader lessons. First, even if companies sell to less cyclical industries, steady revenue streams from flow products are typically more attractive than those dependent on capex. Partly, this is due to the fact there is often more pronounced cyclicality in capex spending than many investors estimate. If economic uncertainty runs high, all kinds of customers hold back on spending. The lesser predictability is undesirable.

Second, spending on flow products tends to invite less customer scrutiny. Capital investments, whether on a drilling rig or a new office building, always receive serious price attention. Flow products, on the other hand, slip more easily below the radar because of their smaller size and greater regularity.

THE SILENT ASSASSIN: CUSTOMER CYCLICALITY

Cyclicality can change customer behavior in unpredictable ways. During flush periods, companies spend. Budgets are generous and getting quality equipment and services delivered on time takes precedence over cost. But when times turn tough, cost consciousness rises. Besides initial cutbacks to capital expenditure, most companies reexamine their cost structures.

Many find they have been overpaying suppliers. After all, most suppliers to cyclical industries are adept at aligning pricing with customers' budgeting. Some customers even demand across the board supplier price cuts. Amid plummeting oil prices in late 2014, for example, E&P company Statoil demanded a 20% price cut from all suppliers. The effect is to neutralize pricing power.

Downturns can even affect flow products. Some customers cut costs by stretching out equipment maintenance schedules and deferring overhauls or repairs. Some move to self-service maintenance or increase use of non-original spare parts. Companies can become more inclined to buy equipment or services from second tier providers, sacrificing reliability for cost.

If these changes were transient they would not necessarily pose a big problem, but they often become permanent. A recent example occurred in the air-freight industry. Over recent decades, many companies developed the habit of shipping certain goods by air, which is faster but far more costly than shipping by sea. When the global financial crisis hit, many shifted back to sea freight. They found that, with minor adjustments, their supply chain could function equally well with a substantially smaller component of goods shipped by air. Even when good times returned, they saw no reason to revert.

LONG PERIOD SWELLS

Cyclicality's underpinnings can be murky, especially when expansionary periods (the swells) are sustained for a surprisingly long time. People begin to believe that cyclicality has been conquered, and growth starts to look sustainable even when it is not. After all, cyclicality is not something companies like to admit to. If things stay good enough for longer than usual, they are inclined to perceive the great performance as the 'new normal'.

An acute problem with no-cyclicality arguments, however, is that they are the most dangerous when they look most reasonable. When expansionary periods last longer than before, companies exposed to the cycle will look the most compelling. Their five-year and even ten-year track records can look so strong as to make it seem illogical to consider what occurred 20 years earlier.

A more pernicious situation arises when companies that don't necessarily seem cyclically exposed start to benefit from cyclicality. Unsustainable booms in certain countries or industries can benefit companies that normally wouldn't be exposed to such effects.

Distinguishing between sustainable structural growth for a company and mere cyclicality is not always easy. If growth in a historically stable company gradually increases, it is easier to assume that higher structural growth rates or market share gains are driving it than that cyclicality has crept into the equation. Sustainably higher growth has a different effect on a quality company's future value creation than a cyclical growth spurt. Underestimating the cyclical effects can therefore impact materially on investment performance.

SAIPEM: LONG PERIOD SWELLS

In the fall of 2012, during a period of high but stable oil prices, we bought shares in Saipem, an offshore oilfield services company with origins dating to the 1950s when it began as a division of Eni. Upstream exploration and production spending had increased at a rapid clip for a decade – a 17% compound annual growth rate – and capital was flowing to develop increasingly harder-to-reach oil fields. For a decade, Saipem boasted double-digit growth in earnings and strong returns on capital.

The Economist called offshore oil services companies like Saipem "the unsung masters of the industry."[34] Rising demand emanated from emerging markets. Supply was limited outside of core OPEC countries, thanks to high marginal costs of production and an industry habit of lagged response to higher prices. Years of under-investment in new capacity tightened the demand-supply equation. According to our quality investing philosophy, Saipem looked good.

As soon as the end of 2012, however, signs of deterioration in these economically appealing trends were increasingly evident. On the demand side, consumers were becoming intolerant of high oil prices; on the supply side, US shale oil production was emerging as a cheaper and reliable substitute for traditional crude oil. Suppliers faced increased cost pressures and delivery overruns for new build projects. Industry-wide returns faltered.

Shareholder pressure prompted oil companies to reduce planned capital expenditures, cutting revenue for oil service companies, such as Saipem, just after they had invested considerable capital to expand. Before year-end 2012, Saipem disclosed execution problems with numerous ongoing projects, and that it would miss its yearly targets. For the next three years, the company continued to downgrade expectations and over that time lost nearly 80% of its market value. We sold the stock early in the downturn, but not before taking a loss.

Our costly error was mistaking cyclical growth for structural growth. We had underappreciated the extremely protracted nature of cycles in the natural resources industry. A more comprehensive analysis extending back to the early 1980s, the most recent analogous period, would have highlighted how the oil and gas industry was engaged in a historically massive capacity build-out program. The stimulus was historically high oil prices; in inflation-adjusted terms, the price of oil had only been higher on one occasion in the preceding 100 years.

This example offers numerous lessons about cyclicality. For one, cycles can vary enormously in length: for some industries, ten or even 20 years of history provides insufficient context. To gauge this, and help improve the understanding of a cyclical company through the cycle, it is important to analyze the information available as far back as possible, preferably several decades.

Further, while focusing our analysis on demand, the driver of sales growth, we had ignored the axiom that it is usually supply that arrests profit growth in cyclical industries. When capacity is tight, the backlog grows at double-digit rates, and the company can name its price. An investor is unlikely to notice that some projects are being executed poorly, key people are leaving, or new contracts are too risky.

Above all, while phrases like "demand super-cycle" sound like the foundation for an intelligent argument, they are euphemisms for the foolish belief that good times will last forever. When cyclical industries falter, many analysts portray it as a natural or even healthy adjustment period. They say it may be painful, but it will end. Yet when the cycle turns up, the talk is of permanent trends and why *this* upturn is different, and more durable, often using puffy adages such as "all the easy oil has been drilled." In flush periods, such narratives can be seductive. But for highly cyclical industries, it is when prospects look brightest that investors should be most wary.

ANALYTICAL PROBLEMS

Cyclicality poses several analytical problems. Amid cycle peaks, revenue growth rates and margins are usually elevated, but it is difficult to be sure by how much. In theory, the level could be inferred by computing the long-run average over a lengthy period covering multiple cycles. Trouble is, such long periods are often dynamic, with changes in the company, industry, and economy, so the measures may be incomparable. Even the companies themselves have difficulty discerning how specific changes in context relate to resulting profit levels.

For industries that are closely linked to a particular commodity, the challenge gets even tougher. Activity levels for a company selling into the oil and gas industry will look very different if the new normal price for crude oil is $50 per barrel versus $100 per barrel. When buying companies with a strong commodity link, direct or indirect, an investor makes an implicit bet on the commodity price. We urge caution. History teaches that it is easy to have an intelligent opinion about commodity prices, but tough to get it right.

Finally, although time is the investor's friend with stable companies, time can be an enemy concerning cyclical companies. When a company grows its business and profits consistently every year, an investor can relax and enjoy the beauty of compounding. Enter cyclicality, and investors can face long periods of stagnant or declining profits. This increases the importance of timing, with results being more dependent on when positions are bought and sold. Timing investments in cyclical companies is never easy, but we try to understand the specific cycles to which our companies are exposed to the greatest extent possible. This helps us to mitigate risks and increases the chances that we can capitalize on the periods of growth.

A SILVER LINING: THE STRONG GET STRONGER

There is a silver lining with cyclicality. Big changes tend to favor quality companies over weaker counterparts. With superior products, better economic characteristics, and often stronger management, they can often capitalize on the challenges of cyclicality.

Investments by a business are more valuable when they are countercyclical. Being able to invest in products, customer relationships, and advertising when others must scale back usually translates into stronger market positions over the long run. Being able to do deals when competitors are preoccupied with other concerns likewise tends to produce gains.

During the 2008 financial crisis, for instance, while vast portions of the business community were paralyzed, quality companies tended to buy, invest, and expand at low cost amid plentiful opportunities. The investments and effort they put in during the challenging years translated into better businesses with stronger competitive advantages, market shares, and economic characteristics than before the crisis. Exemplars include many of the investments made by Warren Buffett and Berkshire Hathaway during the depths of the credit crisis of 2008, including extremely lucrative convertible preferred stock in General Electric (US) and Goldman Sachs, and a valuable option to acquire a sizable minority stake in Bank of America. The important lesson for investors is that the value of owning the highest quality company rises with cyclicality, as these companies tend to be better equipped to deal with it and capitalize on it.

B. TECHNOLOGICAL INNOVATION

The word innovation carries positive connotations, along with gratitude toward great inventors who have improved life, such as Alexander Fleming's discovery of penicillin, Thomas Alva Edison's light bulb and Robert Noyce's integrated circuit. But, at least for capitalists, innovation is two-edged: while great improvements create new fortunes and even new industries, they often decimate others.

Innovation can be such a brutal and destructive force for businesses that we often avoid industries where the risk of significant technological innovation is high. Among the most important questions we ask when investing is whether a company's products will still exist in a similar and relevant form ten years hence.

Asking this question doesn't solve all problems. Indeed buying a manufacturer of fax machines would probably have looked sensible until well into the 1990s. Even so, we still think asking the basic question reduces the temptation to wade into areas where rapid innovation is at play and is therefore likely to hurt us. Below we look at some of the risks associated with large-scale innovation and those industries characterized by high-paced innovation.

A cautionary stance on these types of innovation is why our investments are more tilted towards optically stodgier areas like elevators and cosmetics rather than electronics and e-commerce. People will want to travel safely down buildings even if they work for Amazon, and as long as people want to look good, they will buy cosmetics.

Scaling innovation risk

Small-scale innovation, like improved product packaging or safety, usually adds value and poses modest risk. It is large-scale innovation that can be perilous. Such innovation means disruption of existing economic models. Profit pools can rapidly shift from established companies to new ones. With every shake up, some great businesses are destroyed while others flourish. But it is usually easier to identify innovation's losers well before picking the long-term winners.

In the news business, for example, it has long been evident that the ongoing trend toward online content would disrupt the economics of print newspaper publishers but even today it is not entirely clear how the historical profit pool will be split among consumers, new entrants, and incumbents. The same thing is happening in large parts of retailing with the emergence of dominant stars like Amazon.

As Harvard Business School Professor Clayton M. Christensen elucidates in *The Innovator's Dilemma*, even the most historically attractive business models can be shattered by innovation upheaval. While participants can invariably offer reasons why given changes are manageable or even present opportunities, we maintain a healthy skepticism. When momentous innovation rocks established industries, companies soon face frustrating choices. Infrastructure built around a certain method must be changed, yet it is not always obvious how to adapt. In the news business, for example, the trade-off – still unresolved – centers around whether to put online content behind paywalls, offer it free, or use some tiered combination. For traditional retailers, balancing store network pricing and mix with online pricing and mix remains perplexing.

Big innovation results in more victims than victors, despite what incumbent industry leaders might assert. Exceptions to the historical pattern are rare so we are not patient with arguments about why this time or this industry is different.

FAST-PACED INNOVATION

Industries with high innovation rates are especially unpredictable. Even the best-positioned firm in a rapidly changing operating environment can easily be toppled. Given the unpredictable nature of rapid innovation, industries prone to it are unlikely to contain many quality companies. Such industries are more like lotteries, where a few stock pickers may get lucky once in a while but most lose out.

NOKIA: FAST-PACED INNOVATION

"I have learned that we are standing on a burning platform," stated an unusually frank memo from the Chief Executive of an iconic company to his staff in February 2011. "There is intense heat coming from our competitors, more rapidly than we ever expected... We fell behind, we missed big trends, and we lost time."

Nokia's origins date to 1865, when Fredrik Idestam set up a wood pulp mill in South-West Finland. Following forays into industries ranging from Wellington boots to chemicals, the company introduced its first mobile phone in 1987. By 1998 it had overtaken Motorola to become the global leader in the sector, and by 2007, Nokia's share of the phone market ran to 40%. This attractive share growth combined with an expanding market drove the company's market capitalization ever higher, at one point hitting €110bn.

Shortly after this, the company's seemingly inexorable rise was halted by a three-pronged attack from companies not previously considered competitors. Apple shipped the first iPhone in 2007, and by 2010 its market share grew to 61% of the high-end smartphone market. In two years, Google's operating system Android attracted an ecosystem of software and hardware developers which helped Samsung to capture market share of medium priced smartphones. In the low-end price range, low cost semi-conductors allowed manufacturers in China to capture more than a third of the phones sold globally. By 2012, Nokia's handset business suffered operating losses of approximately €2bn, and in September 2013, Nokia announced that it would exit the business.

This is a relatively well-known story and much has been made of the Nokia case study, with various analysts blaming the company's inability to take risks or to make decisions quickly. However, many companies are relatively risk averse, or have a slow decision-making process. The vast majority have not experienced a comparable collapse in profitability and market value. While it's always tempting to seek answers inside the company, and blame corporate culture or poor strategic decisions, here the main culprit is the industry itself.

Unlike, for example, the elevator industry or liquor business, the consumer electronics sector is prone to rapid technological discontinuities. Whether it's a switch from CD players to MP3 players, from DVD rentals to online streaming, or from analogue mobile phones to smartphones, changes happen quickly and the direction of the switch is only ever obvious in hindsight.

There is no expensive infrastructure to replace, or long-term contracts to provide security – consumers can just walk into the store one day and buy the new product. Incumbents usually struggle to respond successfully to the disruption; both because they've built the organization and cost structure around the old technology, and because it takes time to learn a new technology or business model. The consumer electronics industry is also prone to commoditization, as the technology becomes more standardized and imitators willing to take a lower margin enter the market.

Nokia may have done plenty of things right, but even a more nimble corporate culture would have been unable to arrest the momentum that Apple's and Google's ecosystems had gained. Sustaining market leadership in industries marked by fast-paced innovation is extremely challenging – which makes us wary of investing in such sectors, despite the spectacular growth that can be achieved.

C. DEPENDENCY

Whenever a company depends significantly on factors outside its control, risk rises. These factors become important when they can significantly alter the competitive advantage or economics of the business. In this section we examine the issues associated with dependency on government policy or contracts before looking at some of the ways that stakeholder concentration or dependency on an unstable industry structure can increase the risks for an investor.

GOVERNMENTS

We are wary of businesses where governments play a large role in determining corporate fortunes. Government actions, which are political and therefore often unpredictable, can both catapult a business to prosperity and cut it down.

The issue is acute for companies that rely on fixed infrastructure, such as telecom operators, utility and oil producers, and mining companies. Since wiring, power plants, oil wells, and mines cannot readily be moved, governmental impositions – from carbon taxes to excise taxes on oil and mineral extraction – are neither predictable nor avoidable.

Complacency about the role of government can arise when policies make a business artificially strong. Take the renewable energy industry in large parts of Europe. Before the global financial crisis began in 2008, generous government subsidies led many companies to think the renewable energy business offered great returns. The subsidies benefitted the companies building vast solar parks and wind farms, and also created a tremendous boom for suppliers of everything from wind turbines to silicon wafers.

When times abruptly changed and governments realized they needed to cut costs, subsidies to renewables were ready targets. With a few small government decisions, renewable energy companies from Norway to Portugal went from explosive growth to near bankruptcy. Such episodes, which recur in history, are why government industrial assistance or protection should be viewed as transient, no matter how noble or long-term the government's intentions may seem.

Other scenarios calling for caution are those involving favorable government contracts. Although often lucrative while they last, such arrangements can be changed or renegotiated at government's whim, which often occurs if governments decide they are too favorable to business. The effect caps the economic upside in many areas when the government is counterparty.

This is a perennial problem with government concessions, such as mining contracts. While in theory concession companies are handed monopolies, monopoly-like profitability seldom follows over the long term. Aside from direct power to alter contract terms, government wields an array of tools such as taxes, duties, or regulation that can wipe out contractual advantages.

Businesses whose competitive advantage is tied to prevailing legislation or regulation face particularly serious disruption from policy shifts or changing legal interpretations. Even the most privileged positions can be torn asunder by a change in law.

STAKEHOLDER CONCENTRATION

Strong customer relationships are wonderful but reliance on precious few creates concentration risk. Despite a strong business model and solid historical bonds, such dependency adds uncertainty. As with friendships, business relationships change, often inexplicably. Besides the negative consequences of losing a key customer, the threat of defection confers bargaining power that big customers can use to extract economic concessions that alone or in aggregate may pose significant costs.

Many contemporary challenges facing food and beverage companies arise from their concentrated customer base. Large grocery retailers know their high value to their manufacturers and use it to negotiate lower prices and more favorable terms than they would have gotten otherwise.

Concentration risk extends beyond customers to include suppliers on the production end, who may charge higher prices, and distributors on the sales end, who may offer lower prices. A good example of supplier concentration risk is Safilo, a smaller peer of Luxottica. With more limited retail presence and a narrower portfolio of licensed brands, Safilo has in recent years lost several key licenses, including those of Armani and Polo Ralph Lauren, to Luxottica. Those losses have been costly and the company's stock price has tumbled, lagging the market by more than 80% since the end of 2005.[35]

In some cases, concentration risks include other stakeholders too, such as employees, bankers, and even shareholders. Concentration in any part of a company's value chain harbors hidden risks that can degrade its economics. An example is the impact of Global Distribution Systems (GDS) on the airline industry. Through the 1990s, before the advent of direct internet distribution, GDS became the primary way customers bought airline tickets. Although begun by the airlines, GDS became the gateway to a vast network of travel agents, who along with travelers were the ultimate beneficiaries. While airlines have recovered some ground through direct internet sales from their websites, GDS still generates more than 60% of bookings and 70% of revenues. GDS companies like Spain's Amadeus generate impressive operating margins and considerable returns on capital that dwarf those of most airlines.

New entrants

Business life was easier when national markets were largely closed to outside competitors. In Europe, national corporate champions were able to build business with impressive economics based on market dominance often supported by legacy infrastructure. Free trade agreements and the rise of online commerce have created open marketplaces for virtually all goods and services.

While businesses have always faced the risk of new entrants, building and strengthening competitive advantages were reliable defensive strategies. New entrants are now much harder to fend off. Rivals that previously were not considered a threat can more easily move across borders, virtually or physically. In the UK, for example, the entry of deep-discounters in the grocery market has disrupted what many viewed as an unassailable industry structure.

No company is insulated from competitive onslaughts, but it pays to consider where the threat is more or less acute. Domestic companies already facing significant competition in foreign markets may find those rivals threatening them at home as well. It can be instructive, therefore, to study competitive advantage in a global context, measuring it not only against existing peers in the marketplace but also against a broader competitive set.

D. SHIFTING CUSTOMER PREFERENCES

The economic damage inflicted by shifts in consumer preferences can be severe. When customer preferences change, customer benefits that once provided a competitive advantage can quickly evaporate, threatening even the mightiest of companies. We discuss this below, before taking a more detailed look at the risks of competition from lower-priced, good-enough products.

BENEFIT SWITCH

Companies try to control as many of the variables that influence customer decision making as they can, often through branding and packaging. However, changes in preferences are often associated with variables they cannot control. Take the tobacco industry: companies control taste and nicotine but not public attitudes towards health, which lead some people to quit and others to ostracize those who have not.

In today's food industry, companies likewise grapple with increased interest in nutritional content rather than the historical focus on taste. In retailing, the historical competitive advantage that the consumer benefit of proximity offered is reduced by rising consumer preference for online shopping. No one can control such shifts, but we try to consider them as part of an overall assessment of the durability of competitive advantages.

FASHION RISK

Customer assessments of benefits sometimes change for inscrutable reasons, especially for products offering intangible benefits. Think of how brands seen as cool in the 1980s look hopelessly uncool today or how consumer demand for certain kinds of food or beverages may rise and fall, be it for sodas or red wine. The toy industry has historically been fertile ground for fads to take root and flourish. Examples abound, from the Cabbage Patch Kids dolls and Care Bears of the 1980s to the Tamagotchis and Furbys of the 1990s.

Wholesale revenues from Cabbage Patch Kids dolls, launched by Coleco in 1983, soared to $550 million in 1984, and total merchandise sales brought a multiple of that. A successful pop music record was released and the characters adorned products from clothing to breakfast cereal. The dolls were ubiquitous. By 1987, however, the fad was over, and wholesale revenue dropped by nearly 75%, a collapse that contributed to Coleco's bankruptcy.

Typically such fads are single products or brands whose appeal spikes in one year and then plummets within a few. Generally there is no practical need for the product and often there is some element of associated hype, such as a popular record or other gimmick. While catching a fad early can be lucrative, given stellar initial growth rates, the spectacular fall on the horizon dooms the idea as a long-term investment proposition.

GOOD-ENOUGH GOODS

Premium pricing is a significant source of value creation for many quality companies. By virtue of competitive advantages based on factors such as brand strength, they price products higher than similar alternatives. The strategy's success depends on offering demonstrably greater benefits compared to rival products. We refer to products that rivals push to challenge that advantage as *good-enough goods*.

The leading examples are private label retailer alternatives to branded products, such as those offered by pharmacies and grocers.

By offering similar products at lower prices, chains steer consumers to focus on price rather than quality. Once the switch occurs, customers tend to stick with the private label. Other examples are the low-cost airline industry pioneered by the likes of Ryanair as an alternative to major carriers such as British Airways and open source software, such as Linux, as an alternative to Microsoft Windows.

Good-enough value propositions can be difficult to protect against. On the downside, risk is greater when products are distributed through influential middlemen that command customer respect, such as retailers creating private labels. Such middlemen have economic incentives to create their own good-enough goods. On the other hand, rivals are not invincible and where private label strategies have tried and failed – such as in personal care markets, and segments of the food and beverage industry – it is often a sign of brand strength.

Niche products are typically better protected than large product categories because good-enough goods are likely to require scale to work. Above all, if consumer benefits are genuine and strong, the risk of good-enough competition reduces proportionally. We struggle to see how a good-enough handbag will ever be a credible threat to a branded luxury-goods handbag. Similarly, we doubt that many airlines (or their pilots) would want to fly aircraft with a good-enough engine rather than one with an impeccable record for safety and soundness.

NOBEL BIOCARE: GOOD-ENOUGH GOODS

Dental implants are small titanium screws implanted into a patient's jawbone as the basis for a prosthetic tooth. The technology is relatively new: the first implant was placed in 1965 and the product evolved over the latter part of last century. Before implants, patients that bothered to replace a missing tooth (or teeth) did so with a bridge, a prosthetic which had to be mounted on the remaining teeth either side of the gap. This was a sub-optimal solution for several reasons – not least because these neighboring teeth needed grinding down to accommodate the bridge and often failed themselves after a few years of excessive loading. The implant, while a more invasive procedure, gave a more stable, healthy and better-looking outcome.

At the start of 2007, the prospects for the leading dental implant manufacturers looked fantastic. As a nascent but revolutionary product in a relatively staid industry, the runway for growth was significant. The product had been established for some time, and penetration was increasing from low double-digit percentage levels driven by dentist education programs run by major manufacturers. This had all the hallmarks of a win-win-win business proposition: the consumer was offered a superior solution; dentists were able to make more money from the procedure; and manufacturers were positioned to deliver strong growth at high profitability.

At that time, Nobel Biocare was the leading manufacturer (and marketer) of premium dental implants. Nobel's sales growth averaged in excess of 20% in the four years from 2003, driven by the rapid growth of its sales force, who were able to spend increasing amounts of time with dentists. Product reliability was excellent, with near perfect success rates. Nobel was able to charge premium prices, reflecting product quality and the high level of support they provided to dentists as they started practicing 'implantology'. Alongside, the strong growth, Nobel was delivering stellar returns on capital and impressive margins: gross margins were well above 80% and operating margins reached 34% in 2006.

Nobel seemed to have all the requisite ingredients for a quality investment. Certainly the financial characteristics were strong enough; the potential for further growth was promising and there seemed to be reasonable technological and distribution barriers to entry. We first invested in the business in 2005 and for the first 18 months, things seemed to be playing out as expected. But by the time we exited in early 2008, the position had proven to be a costly mistake.

What went wrong? In a word, competition. The dental implant product is not especially complex. It was possible for other companies to develop similar products and, with incumbents generating gross margins exceeding 80%, challenger companies were able to sell at materially lower prices, while still generating decent profitability. As the category matured, dentists became more familiar with implants. They became more comfortable that the cheaper alternatives – previously dismissed as inferior and less reliable – got the job done.

Dentists no longer relied on the premium-priced brand of the market leader for reassurance. Taking advantage of the consumer's lack of brand awareness, some dentists made higher margins using lower-cost options, by charging the same price for the procedure irrespective of implant used. Since 2007, market volume for implants has expanded, but much of the growth was by lower-cost producers. The premium players ended up reducing their selling price to remain competitive.

None of this is to say that Nobel Biocare is a poor company. It was and remains a good business and was ultimately acquired by Danaher in 2015 (albeit for less than a quarter of its value at the time its 2006 results were published). However, Street forecasts for 2014 (which, due to the Danaher deal, Nobel never actually reported) underline the effect that lower-cost producers had on Nobel's business. Consensus forecasts were for 2014 sales below the 2006 level, with operating margins around 13%. Put another way, pre-tax earnings for 2014 was estimated to be around one-third of the level delivered in 2006. This earnings trajectory occurred as Nobel Biocare's high prices were undercut by competitors whose products may not have been of equivalent quality but proved to be good-enough.

* * *

The factors outlined in this chapter are potential pitfalls for a quality investor because they highlight how attractive financial results often prove to be unsustainable. In the hunt for quality companies, distinguishing between sustainable and unsustainable performance is vital. To minimize the risk of error, it is useful to maintain a systematic process. The next chapter considers how such a process can reduce investing mistakes.

CHAPTER FOUR
IMPLEMENTATION

A N INVESTING STRATEGY THAT IS LONG-TERM and focused on quality faces inexorable challenges, such as resisting temptations to respond to short-term dynamics and standing by qualitative judgments in the face of valuation metrics that can appear elevated. Such challenges can induce corresponding mistakes. Among others, they can allow prevailing macroeconomic conditions to have undue influence on decision-making or induce passing on a unique investment opportunity because of a high earnings multiple.

In this chapter, we analyze the challenges, explore more of the slip-ups we have made, and explain how an investment process might be designed to meet these obstacles and reduce mistakes. Along the way, we discuss valuation and market pricing, explaining why we agree with Charlie Munger, vice chairman of Berkshire Hathaway, that it is better to buy a great company at a fair price, than a fair company at a great price. We also explain why stock markets tend to undervalue quality companies.

A. CHALLENGES

In quality investing, the four most significant challenges are: battling short-term thinking; conquering prevailing preferences for 'hard' numerical data over subjective assessments of quality; accepting that quality companies are not always the most exciting investments; and accepting that quality stocks will often appear to be expensive. We discuss each challenge in turn.

LONG-TERM COMPOUNDING VERSUS SHORT-TERM PRESSURES

One of the greatest challenges of the quality investing philosophy is the need to adopt and sustain a long-term outlook – one measured in years, not quarters or days. In our experience, the best investment results tend to follow from buying and holding quality businesses for the long term.

Yet it is difficult to embrace such an outlook in a business and investment culture that is riveted on short-term outcomes. When participants measure results by the quarter or year, it is unsurprising that managers and investors concentrate on short-term outcomes. For publicly traded companies, the stock market offers a continual reckoning which entices participants to make investment decisions every day. Of late, many are even tempted by flash trading technologies to make such adjustments in matters of minutes or seconds.

Information markets reinforce this temptation. In business and investing, there is invariably incremental information about any stock. Changing information offers the tantalizing prospect of a potential gain from trading in or out. Prevailing culture is reinforced by market volatility – the wide range of highs and lows enticing traders to perceive timing advantages to buy low and sell high. The culture is augmented by sell-side analysts employed by brokers, who add drama by focusing attention on stories of rapid business growth or spectacular turnarounds, narratives that rarely prove to be either useful or true.

Significant short-term market price fluctuations attract attention and dampen appreciation for smaller changes that can lead to significant accumulations over much longer periods. In any given year, compare a stock that soared in price by 50% – some hot tech stock – with one that rose 10% – a stodgy cosmetics maker. Many would wish they were in on the former but care less whether they bought the latter. Yet the latter may offer a far superior long-term proposition.

The concept of compounding is one of the most important and valuable ideas in the world of business and investing. Its power is relatively invisible over short periods of time but galactic over long periods of time. Consider an investment of $10,000 that earns either 10% or 7% annually. During a single year, that amounts to a difference of a mere $300, whereas over a 25-year period, it adds up to $54,000. The 10% annual return results in an investment worth twice as much as that yielding 7%.

A short-term focus may lead investors to reach for companies promising higher earnings growth over shorter periods of time. Suppose a company has for two decades generated earnings growth averaging 9% and paid a 2% dividend, for an all-in return of 11%. If sustainable long term and available at a fair price, such a company would be far more appealing than most. But when investing culture focuses on short-term results, it is tempting to hunt and buy instead a less predictable company touting more rapid near-term earnings growth.

There are also considerable costs to short-term changes, including transactions fees and taxes. But these are not necessarily salient: the fees for single trades may be modest in relation to the size of a trade and are not out of pocket; taxes are often booked and forgotten and paid on the assumption that they are beyond one's control.

So taking the long term is profitable, but challenging. Quality investors must constantly remind themselves that what counts are multi-year periods, not quarters, and that over such long periods of time, the advantage often goes to the plodding and patient rather than the daring and fleet.

It is probably easier for individuals to combat short-termism than institutions, because institutions tend to incubate and reinforce the culture. Institutional clients and their advisors tend to measure their own performance quarterly and annually. Institutional portfolio managers and analysts, catering to such clienteles, do the same. When firms know that the flow of investment funds is determined by quarterly and annual results, managers will put money in investments promising the greatest returns over such periods and analysts will hunt for such opportunities rather than probe which businesses might generate the greatest long-term value.

Battling short-termism requires cultivating the opposite institutional culture with all relevant participants. This includes educating clients, training staff, and creating an appropriate reward structure for decision-makers at the highest level.

LIVING WITH SHORT-TERM
UNDERPERFORMANCE

While a quality investing strategy works over time, periods of underperformance are inevitable. Deeply cyclical sectors lacking strong steady returns on capital or with thin margins are anathema to quality investors. But share prices of such companies often benefit when markets trade certainty for hope. In these industries, small improvements in the macroeconomic environment frequently drive significant improvements in profitability. When markets favor such firms, a quality-focused portfolio will likely deliver comparatively weaker returns.

Although such scenarios are relatively uncommon – perhaps two or three years out of ten[36] – one occurred in 2013 among European equities. Investors scrambled to own any company poised to benefit from a European economic recovery. The upshot? 'Junk' rallied more than quality. Such short-term underperformance is painful while it lasts, but our experience has taught us to stick to our principles. Abandoning an investment philosophy in an effort to benefit from short-term economic data or to participate in market hype seldom leads to good long-term outcomes. On the rare occasions when we tried, it generally led to poor investment outcomes.

More than offsetting periods of underperformance, quality companies have historically fared much better than the market amid economic upheaval. The relative certainty provided by higher margins, stronger returns, greater stability and more robust balance sheets becomes disproportionately valuable. The global financial crisis underscored the point: valuation multiples shrank market-wide, but quality companies outperformed.

QUALITATIVE JUDGMENTS IN A DATA-DRIVEN WORLD

The focus of quality investing on subjective aspects of business presents a challenge in an investing culture more wedded to quantification. So much of investing is numbers-driven: performance is quantified; accounting is numeric; and market moves are stated in percentage terms. The quantitative orientation attracts talented individuals trained to analyze and trust numbers. While a strong quantitative background is an asset for investors, the resulting culture often obscures arguments or rationales based on qualitative analysis.

The process of business analysis usually leads to a set of numerical assessments such as growth forecasts and valuation measures. While they appear to be rigorous assertions of truth, they are riddled with innumerable obscure and subjective judgments, ranging from accounting line items to appropriate discount rates. The figures, in fact, distill many of the building blocks, patterns and pitfalls we have discussed, such as industry structure, pricing power, or cyclicality. Earnings models can also become conduits for the unwitting expression of biases. For example, as an important facet of an investment decision, a model's earnings forecast can be swayed by confirmation bias – the desire to interpret information in a way that confirms an existing hypothesis.

Despite the allure of quantitative data, investors should be aware of their limitations – even while appreciating their utility. The balancing act sometimes poses conundrums, especially when a positive qualitative assessment meets up with elevated price-earnings ratios or negative earnings growth rates. Akin to differences between individuals and institutions concerning time horizon, the tendency to elevate quantitative over qualitative factors is often more pronounced in firms.

The more decision-makers are involved in an investment process, the greater the tendency to distill variegated information into figures, which are easier to circulate, compare, and comment on. Analysts, managers, and directors can defend an investment thesis more readily in terms of earnings per share and price-earnings multiples than by outlining a company's recurring revenues or industrial positioning. It is easier to explain that a stock is cheap than that a company is great.

Being dull in an exciting profession

For many equity investors, stock-picking is like an intellectual treasure hunt: the hope is to discover a company replete with hidden value, a battered trunk full of gold to be unlocked for spectacular returns. This way of thinking dovetails with the notion of market efficiency, where undervalued stocks are both hidden and rare. They require either astute research or at least an elaborate new angle. As such, it is easy to think intelligent investing is the quest for something undiscovered.

Quality companies often lack this cherished pot-of-gold characteristic: they tend not to have products that promise to revolutionize the world. In fact, many of the best companies are simple businesses that have done what they do consistently for decades. Worse, their quality is often, to some extent, already appreciated. Many investors would agree that Hermès or L'Oréal are outstanding companies. A general sense of quality is reflected in their stock prices, which usually trade at a market premium — although one often far lower than we believe that quality is worth.

Nevertheless, modern investors often share a propensity to seek the obscure instead of the obvious, to identify a hot new start-up company, an erstwhile laggard poised for a turnaround, or an emerging competitor threatening to revolutionize an industry. Successful quality investing, therefore, sometimes requires avoiding the temptation of apparently exciting investment discoveries. It means accepting the relative dullness of analyzing what is often in plain view.

B. MISTAKES WHEN BUYING

If smart people learn from their own mistakes while wise people learn from the mistakes of others, the goal is to be both smart and wise. The best thing to do after making or observing a mistake is to acknowledge it and absorb the relevant lessons to avoid repeating it. In the case of quality investing, to paraphrase Mark Twain, while scenarios do not repeat exactly, they do rhyme. This affinity enables us to classify the mistakes we have made or seen into a few categories that, if borne in mind, significantly reduce the probability of future mistakes. We begin with several that plague the initial purchase decision.

TOP-DOWN INTRUSION

Quality investing is best conceived as a 'bottom up' exercise in the sense of focusing primarily on a company and its industry – the firm-specific or microeconomic factors. While many investors share this approach, a good portion also engage in 'top-down' analytics by looking at the broader environment, considering the state of international trade, the rate of inflation, or the relative strengths of currencies.

In a quality investing context, mistakes can arise from elevating top-down perspectives above bottom-up analysis. This kind of error often occurs when large macroeconomic themes start wreaking havoc with stock prices, leading to questions about an investor's exposure to factors such as trade, inflation, or currency values. These macroeconomic trends do warrant close attention as they bear on given companies and industries. However, when top-down factors trump bottom-up analysis, it often leads to choosing companies and industries for the wrong reasons.

A secondary source of mistake risk from top-down investments is weak conviction. Quality investors, inclined to hold for the long term, require the conviction upon purchase to ride out volatility. When an investment idea is predicated on elusive and exogenous forces of macroeconomics, it is far more difficult to have a conviction about a company or even an industry. When adversity or surprise strikes – for example when commodity prices fall or currencies reverse – it can be harder to stand by the thesis. The result is often not only a mistake on buying but a mistake on selling prematurely; even the dreaded syndrome of buying high and selling low.

NEXT-MONDAY OPTIMISM

Optimism is a common source of investing error, plaguing quality investors as much as any other. In the criminal justice system, recidivists often plea for leniency by arguing that they are remorseful and pledging to do better – kick an addiction, get a job, and straighten up. Prosecutors and judges alike would like to believe them, though are often disappointed. In the corporate world, many managerial laggards sing the same tune, stressing that good times are around the corner, assuring investors that problems are behind them and swearing on a new product launch or acquisition. It is tempting to believe in such hopes – which we call *next-Monday optimism* – but they frequently yield mistakes.

Troubled firms and problem-riddled industries are far more likely to stay that way than to recover and scale new heights. Managers and their advisors who strive for a turnaround and present compelling strategies, however, are often convincing enough to induce investor optimism. Good examples recur every decade or so in the case of the airline industry and occurred in the steel industry for a few years at the start of the 21st century.

Most next-Monday industries and companies continue to disappoint because their infirmities are due to external factors that no management can permanently overcome. While turn-around or restructuring programs may create windows of opportunity for incremental improvement, broader industry conditions ultimately prevail. Even for investors able to pinpoint the time when a structurally challenged industry is due its moment in the sun, they still must time the sunset. That means timing both the decision to buy and the decision to sell, which makes mistakes twice as likely.

Overconfidence

Overconfidence is the root cause of many mistakes. Some individuals may command the relevant background knowledge to credibly evaluate most leading companies in at least a few industries. But even this does not eliminate risks of overconfidence. People are inclined to overestimate their knowledge and abilities, whether in driving or romance. In investing, overconfidence manifests in many ways, not least the reliance placed on specific earnings forecasts despite their inherent limitations.

Straying beyond the boundaries of one's knowledge and experience increases the risk of error. For instance, any investment in a stock that depends on the outcome of external factors beyond a company's control is on shaky ground. Examples of such buys are a pharmaceutical company on the assumption of forthcoming approval of a drug; a gaming company on the belief that authorizing legislation will be enacted; a mining company because iron ore prices are likely to rise. Given the arbitrary nature of many political decisions, even the most expert analysts struggle to predict how a government's actions might impact a particular stock. The same is true of companies with exposure to commodity prices. As a result, where these variables are present, the chance of making erroneous forecasts increases.

Many investing mistakes arise from an illusion of predictability, which are especially acute in any rapidly-changing industry, such as technology. An investor may command considerable knowledge of a given tech-driven industry – whether artificial intelligence or robotics – that facilitates reliable evaluation of the short-term performance and prospects of the companies operating within that sector. Beyond that, factors of dynamism and fluidity degrade forecasting reliability.

The illusion of predictability also seems to recur in companies that are organizationally complex, such as industrial conglomerates or diversified financial institutions. Such companies may well be accessible to the student of industry or finance and even manifest features associated with quality companies, but their sheer scale and inherent opacity can lead even experts to perceive predictability that is partial at best. For example, Siemens operates through 19 divisions ranging from smart grid, to medical diagnostics and industry automation. While it is tempting to evaluate whether Siemens is a quality company, its enormity and intricacy presents considerable risks of mistake.

Insisting on a firm basis of knowledge about a company and its industry, and being alert to the risks of straying into unfamiliar territory, is important. When this sound foundation exists, interpreting and responding to surprise events or disruptions is more likely to be done rationally. Being aware of the risks of overconfidence is an equally important step: in a well-known sector, the danger of overestimating one's ability to forecast is most acute.

DEBT

Many investing mistakes can be traced to overlooking the downside risks of debt or its sources. Debt can be seductive because even investors wary of excessive leverage can be deceived into stressing its upside more than its downside. After all, leverage can readily be rationalized, with managers and advisors alike explaining how unconventionally high debt levels are either under unusually tight control or insulated from the usual risks of calamity amid business adversity.

Debt brings varying interest rates, restrictive loan covenants, and scheduled due dates that put considerable control over value creation in the hands of lenders rather than managers, to the detriment of owners. Risks are particularly great for companies exposed to cyclical end markets. Since cycles invariably defy expectations, borrowers and lenders alike often miscalculate the line between reasonable and excessive leverage.

Drastic mistakes regarding debt levels congregate in two related situations. The first are companies that combine substantial financial debt with high operating leverage. Amid periods of economic expansion, the operating leverage enables growing revenue at lower cost, enabling cash flows that comfortably cover repayment of borrowed money. But in economic downturns, high operating leverage readily translates into rapidly deteriorating cash flows and difficulty meeting debt obligations. Overlooking this feature of debt is a trap for the unwary and one that even experienced investors are prone to fall into.

A second place where debt poses elevated risk of mistakes concerns companies heavily reliant on leases, such as retailers. When retailers grow rapidly during economic expansions, growth often includes adding stores using leased spaces. During such periods, it is easy to overlook that such leases are a source of leverage. When economic conditions contract, the lease rates remain the same while revenue and cash flows decline.

More generally, debt-oriented mistakes are most likely during periods of economic expansion. Amid prosperity, even mediocre companies appear to perform exceptionally well. During such frothy periods, market valuations tend to be high and it can be tempting to compromise on issues such as leverage. Such an environment breeds mistakes, few more dangerous than overlooking the downside and sources of debt.

C. MISTAKES OF RETENTION

Since quality investing entails owning the best companies for the long term, mistakes can occur due to complacency and failure to appreciate when a once-great company is falling from grace. We refer to this as the problem of *boiling frogs*, referencing the experiments which purported to demonstrate that frogs dropped in boiling water promptly jump out but those placed in cool water whose temperature is gradually raised to boiling remain in the scalding caldron. (We recognize the irony that this premise was subsequently proven to be false.) No company is invincible and we devote considerable effort to monitoring and noticing signs of deterioration to enable us to jump out of the pot before being boiled. In addition to the problem of the boiling frog, the following section discusses mistakes of myopia, rationalization, and developing emotional attachment to investments.

BOILING FROGS

Companies rarely deteriorate from great to good in a single quarter or year, but rather decline gradually over a few years or more. There is seldom a single defining moment when it becomes obvious that a business has gone from high quality to low. In the rare cases when decline is rapid and clear, it is easy to sell as quickly as a frog might jump from boiling water. In most cases, it is necessary to develop a means to discern the gradual decay and, especially, to resist complacency and denial in the face of gathering adversity.

For instance, a profit warning is potentially a symptom of deep-seated problems. Our own research among European companies indicates that one-third of those issuing large profit warnings (measured as causing a stock price drop exceeding 10%) issued another, usually larger, profit warning within one year.[37]

A material profit warning, even from a company in a relatively stable industry, can indicate that serious internal problems are brewing, suggesting a need to fully reevaluate the investment thesis. The fact that one profit warning increases the chances of another one also raises questions of how much of a company's stock to own, even where we are confident that no structural changes have occurred to the investment thesis.

For many fallen angels, overall deterioration generally begins with small things not going according to plan: growth not materializing, unexplained pressure on margins, more discussion of competitive pressures, or gradual increases in capital expenditure. Each disappointment is small in isolation; management provides a good explanation for each and dismisses them as non-recurring. But a string of setbacks often signals a larger set of problems, which emerge or crystallize after it is too late for the business to make corrections or for the investor to mitigate losses. Thus even small setbacks warrant rigorous evaluation.

TESCO: BOILING FROG

For many years, Tesco was the darling of the UK food retail industry. In an incredible run from 1995 to 2007, its UK market share doubled to exceed 30%, twice that of its nearest rival. Tesco also developed a huge non-food operation, pioneered online food retailing, and created enormous, profitable international operations. The company consistently increased sales at a double-digit rate and was regularly cited as a paragon of operational excellence.

When we invested in the company in 2007, Tesco's market leadership seemed to confer competitive advantages that would let it continue taking market share and expanding successfully overseas. That proved incorrect. Tesco's UK market share has fallen substantially; margins have declined from 6% to 1%; UK operating profit is one-fifth what it was in its best years; and it made a $400 million accounting error in 2014. What went so wrong at this feted market leader?

For one, overzealous foreign expansion. Tesco was confident in its ability to develop operations in overseas markets, primarily in Asia and Eastern Europe. In triumphant roll-outs, Tesco built huge supermarkets which attracted customers from less developed retailers and more traditional channels. The potential for retail growth in these markets was and remains substantial. If Tesco could grow fast enough to achieve scale, management believed it could replicate its winning UK model.

The expansion was huge: in two decades, Tesco transformed from being primarily a UK supermarket to having two-thirds of its floor space and one-third of group sales abroad. Such rapid and robust growth was presumably exciting for the management team, but drained focus, management resources, and capital. Many ventures did not generate the expected return on capital levels, prompting Tesco to close, sell, or curtail operations worldwide, including in China, Japan, and the US.

In the UK a benign competitive environment was about to change as rivals roared back after conquering festering problems – Morrisons finally digested its Safeway acquisition while Sainsbury's and Asda improved their execution – and the deep discounters such as Aldi and Lidl emerged. Tesco ceded ground to the resurgent competition, letting operating margin rise at the expense of investment in its customers, while allocating the excess capital to overseas expansion. Domestic competitors expanded store footprints at a faster rate than the market grew, at the same time as the deep discounters grabbed nearly 10% of the UK grocery market.

Tellingly, in 2011, long-standing CEO Terry Leahy left Tesco, at the height of the company's UK stature. Today, Tesco gets low marks from UK consumers, ranking dead last in a June 2015 survey about favorite grocers that underscores the deep damage done to the brand.[38] It was easy to underestimate the cumulative impact of a confluence of negative factors – overzealous expansion, loss of focus on core UK consumers, and inadequate response to competitive onslaught – that meant weak business performance at Tesco and poor returns for investors. We sold the last of our shares in mid-2012 before the worst of Tesco's troubles manifested in 2014, but the frog was already well on its way to being boiled by the time we exited.

Ignoring changes to the marketplace

Since quality investing chooses great companies for long-term ownership, complacency amid adversity is fertile ground for mistakes of omission; in other words failing to sell ahead of decline. It is tempting to interpret adversity as transient – to see sagging growth as a blip rather than structural, or a new competitor as unthreatening to a company's core business. This attitude promotes a long-term view but can create blind spots. While each change warrants individual scrutiny, a few categories of change seem to account for a large portion of mistakes.

Firstly, technological changes driving market alterations are often more serious than they initially seem, especially in consumer or retail channels. The Yellow Pages companies from America to Europe went from virtual monopolies to business dinosaurs within a few years. This teaches us to scrutinize and question a company's ability to make the changes necessary to protect its business model.

Secondly, business downturns from changing economic environments tend to be more protracted than anticipated. Any company forecasting improvements several quarters into the future despite a choppy near term is conveying hope not facts. Few industries go from boom to bust and back in less than 12 months.

Finally, if a company's customers are getting poorer, the company will soon follow, as struggling customers reduce budgets. A German manufacturer of bank ATM machines, Wincor Nixdorf, assured investors of continued prosperity as the 2008 financial crisis dawned since credit market turmoil did not bear on cash dispensing. But as faltering banks cut costs, they bought far fewer ATMs.

Thesis creep and "yes, but" mistakes

Mistakes often originate in how investors defend a decision to retain ownership of a stock. In our regular portfolio reviews, for example, one colleague plays devil's advocate to challenge another on the merits of an existing holding. As the proponent engages with the critique, everyone listens for a "yes, but" – an acknowledgement of difficulty followed by a negating qualification.

When the argument for holding a position starts with a "yes, but", it often means both that a mistake has been identified and that someone is unwilling to admit that. Often, a "yes, but" response shifts the investment thesis for retention from bottom-up quality investing to top-down variables – the mistake of top-down intrusion noted earlier.

Two common variations of top-down intrusion are "yes, but": "the market is on top of the issue now"; or "the stock is cheap now." But both statements indicate thesis creep and are also usually truisms: if a company has highlighted a problem, the market knows about it; and its price-earnings multiple will have accordingly contracted. Many investment mistakes of retention follow such special pleading: if a position is maintained as a result of "yes, buts" it is probably a mistake.

ACCOUNTING RED FLAGS

As the language of business, every investor must be conversant in accounting. Beyond assessing fundamentals of asset turns and margins to evaluate business quality, financial reports often contain innumerable subtle clues about the sustainability and predictability of earnings growth, cash flows, and returns on capital. They also occasionally reveal chicanery, eliminating a company from contention as a quality investment.

A perennial challenge that investors face is earnings management, which a 2012 academic study found is pervasive: one-in-five public companies misrepresent earnings by an average of 10%.[39] Accounting shenanigans can manifest in many ways, including premature revenue recognition,[40] inflated gross margins,[41] improperly capitalized expenses,[42] depleting reserves,[43] and manipulating cash flows.[44] Many of these areas include some degree of judgment. However, when these judgments start to move beyond the realms of reasonableness, our experience is that it is usually a mistake to ignore them: such accounting red flags can be powerful indicators that the underlying business is also deteriorating.

ELEKTA: ACCOUNTING RED FLAGS

Elekta was founded in the early 1970s by Lars Leksell, a Swedish Professor of Neurosurgery credited with inventing radio surgery. The company's main business is the sale and servicing of radiotherapy machines designed to precisely deliver radiation doses to shrink tumors and kill cancer cells.

The business has many attributes warranting strong consideration by a quality investor. It generates considerable recurring revenue; demonstrates excellent R&D capabilities; steadily gained market share in an oligopoly; and seemed to have cracked the code for successful expansion into new markets. These characteristics supported a stellar historical track record of sales and earnings growth, well into double digits, and a share price that rose in tandem – it increased 15-fold in a decade through 2013.

Yet something in the company's financial statements seemed odd, suggesting that Elekta's real revenue growth was lower than reported. They saw a sharp deterioration in the portion of reported revenue being converted into ultimate cash flows.

Looking closer, there was a substantial rise in unbilled accrued income, increasing at a rate well ahead of reported top-line growth. Beginning in 2012, the company seemed to be recording a rising proportion of revenues earlier than usual, including by booking sales immediately upon product shipment rather than upon customer receipt and billing. Such changes are red flags because they expand managerial discretion over revenue recognition.

Moreover, we found that accounts receivables were growing faster than sales indicating that the company might have extended payment terms to benefit sales growth or that the company was taking on increased customer payment risk. The combination of rising revenue recognized before billing and subsequent payment delays after billing signaled deteriorating revenue quality.

In addition, it also appeared that Elekta was capitalizing a growing proportion of its R&D spending, meaning deferring the recognition of expenses from the current period to future periods. While that boosts today's bottom line, the charges eventually show up. There can be honest rationales for capitalizing R&D, such as better matching of expense to revenue, but when combined with the other accounting red flags, it aroused suspicion.

Finally, we noticed material insider share-selling by a member of Elekta's senior management during 2012 and 2013. It was time to sell, and the timing proved propitious. Over the ensuing two years, as underlying problems were revealed, the company's share price tumbled. Accounting red flags often signal trouble ahead for a company. Investors beware.

THE ENDOWMENT EFFECT

The quality investing method of conducting rigorous fundamental analysis and holding for the long term creates one final pool of mistakes arising from what behavioral economists call the endowment effect – an over-appreciation of things already owned compared to other opportunities.

Quality investing is particularly susceptible because the considerable upfront research and extensive winnowing increases the endowment effect – the investor's sense of ownership encompasses not just the stock but also their analysis and judgment. The emotional connection amplifies with time, increasing susceptibility the longer a stock is owned. The endowment effect may manifest itself when an investor continues to own a stock despite a drumbeat of negative events revealing a deterioration of the company's fundamental economic characteristics. One strategy to combat this is to ask whether, with a fresh start, you would still buy the same company today.

As with other sources of challenges and mistakes catalogued in this chapter, the endowment effect also plays a positive role in quality investing. It strengthens resolve amid relentless but erroneous pressures to sell. The competing factors therefore call for alertness above all. A long-term strategy must be finely balanced against the recognition that things can, and will, change. All companies evolve to some extent and closely monitoring such evolution is an essential part of the investment process.

D. VALUATION AND MARKET PRICING

Valuations can be powerful: if an analyst determines that something is cheap it is tempting to buy, period, even though the valuation is only an estimate and the company may face challenges from industry forces or competitive pressures. A quality investing strategy, therefore, emphasizes quality first, and valuation second.[45] In this section, we highlight some drawbacks of traditional valuation approaches, before explaining why we believe markets tend to under-value quality companies.

LIMITATIONS OF TRADITIONAL VALUATION APPROACHES

For most of the past decade, Novo Nordisk's shares appeared pricey relative to its sector and the market, trading in the vicinity of 20 times earnings. Despite this optically expensive multiple, investing at almost any point during the decade would have been lucrative. Financial analysts' models routinely underestimated the earnings growth driven by Novo's attractive and stable financial and corporate characteristics. The Novo example, one of many, illustrates the rationality of prioritizing analysis of corporate quality over valuation.

Typical valuation models, such as discounted cash flow (DCF), are riddled with limitations, even for companies with predictable cash flows. Most strikingly, DCF models are constrained by a powerful anchoring effect of prevailing market prices. If analysis indicates a valuation significantly different from market price – say 30% above or below – you can be sure the sell-side analyst will return to the drawing board and adjust some assumptions. Such tendencies cast doubt on the objectivity of many DCF exercises. And experience repeatedly suggests that such anchoring is flawed. Take L'Oréal, which in 1990 boasted a market capitalization of less than $5 billion. Even using extreme growth assumptions, few would have forecasted that L'Oréal, 25 years later, would be worth more than $110 billion.

In short, while quality investing – like other strategies, most notably value investing – prefers to buy at prices below value, it is allergic to 'bargains' unless fundamental bottom-up analysis supports the investment thesis. Concomitantly, when investors rivet on value, there is a tendency to put too much weight on the result, to interpret what is clearly an estimate as hard fact, and thus to miss opportunities such as L'Oréal. No investor wishes to pay more than fair value for a stock, but putting quality ahead of valuation helps us to seize the long-term opportunity.

The insufficient valuation premium for quality

In quality investing, as in any investment strategy, the risk of overpayment exists, but far less than one might think. At a glance, the price-earnings multiples of a quality business relative to its growth can look exaggerated. There are usually plenty of companies that trade on lower multiples and with seemingly higher growth rates. *Seemingly*, because in equity markets, there can be a big difference between expected growth and realized growth. Expert estimates are consistently wrong in aggregate, routinely by more than 10%. Crucially, quality companies tend to exceed estimates, meeting or beating forecasts far more frequently than inferior rivals.[46]

When investors perceive valuation multiples of quality companies to be too high, we refer to the companies as tomorrow stocks. Many investors might agree that some of the companies we have been illustrating are great companies. They just want them cheaper and wait until 'tomorrow', when the price might decline.

The problem is that the day seldom comes: if a company keeps delivering operationally, its relative valuation multiple rarely contracts. If such a day does come, it is usually in the midst of the turmoil of a major market correction. While seizing purchase opportunities in such environments is lucrative, it is equally rational to buy quality companies when valuations are attractive enough, despite seemingly high multiples. Just ask the many thousands of investors who have passed on buying Berkshire Hathaway shares – today priced at more than $200,000 – at any time since 1965.

The risk of overpayment is also offset by a general tendency of stock markets to under-price quality companies.[47] Share prices, even when at seemingly high valuation multiples, often fail to fully capture the combination of predictability and value creation such companies offer. Explanations for this phenomenon include market incentives skewed to the short term, a pervasive presumption of mean reversion that does not automatically apply to well-positioned companies, and an under-appreciation of earnings upside for quality companies[48]. Let's take each of these in turn and consider them in more detail.

Quality companies thrive long term but stock markets tend to overweight the short term. Investors, analysts, and fund managers are evaluated and rewarded quarterly or annually. They respond accordingly, by hunting for stocks that will outperform the market in the coming quarters or year or two. This near-term focus manifests itself in the declining average stock-holding periods of US mutual funds, which have shortened from over six years in the 1950s and 1960s to less than a year more recently.[49] It is also apparent from comparing what moves market prices versus what drives long-term value. Although on a one-year view, nearly 80% of stock price moves are explained by changes in multiples,[50] the driver of longer-term stock returns is earnings growth. For investors seeking to profit in the stock market over the short term, the 80% figure underlines the importance to them of determining the right valuation multiple. Consequently every bit of information that might justify a change in a stock's multiple, however insignificant, is scrutinized, while longer-term earnings power and predictability is subordinated.

Another factor behind general under-pricing of quality is the widespread assumption in finance of mean reversion – that above-average levels of either growth or return on capital must return to average.[51] We concur with the numerous studies providing strong evidence of pervasive mean reversion in business and a general tendency for abnormal returns to erode, but that does not warrant applying the assumption indiscriminately to all industries and companies.

While businesses facing open and competitive markets are almost certainly unable to sustain abnormally high performance, those benefitting from the patterns of quality companies do not necessarily face such headwinds – whether this is due to recurring revenues, friendly middlemen, toll roads, pricing power, brand strength or the others we have catalogued. In such cases, superior cash flows, margins, returns, and growth can be sustained, and even improved, over long periods of time. Focusing on such businesses reduces the chances of error in cash flow forecasting and therefore the risk of permanent loss of capital. Such an approach does not prevent error or loss, of course, but reducing the frequency and severity of losses is as important to long-term returns as picking winners.

Companies that are consistently able to deploy cash at high incremental rates of return often exceed earnings expectations over the long term. So, while the valuation premiums of such companies may reflect solid expected operational performance, they often underestimate actual performance. Thus, stock prices tend to undervalue quality companies.

E. INVESTMENT PROCESS AND MISTAKE REDUCTION

The better an investor knows a business, the better the ensuing investment decisions tend to be. Therefore, the starting point is detailed fundamental analysis. The aim should be to get to know a business better than anyone who is not an insider. There are few shortcuts and this process involves a meticulous review of all public information, such as financial reports, as well as mining other independent sources, including competitors, customers, suppliers and former employees.

A basic tenet of intellectual inquiry is to attack a subject from multiple angles in order to form a full picture of a target investment. This attitude was developed by Philip Fisher as the "scuttlebutt method" in his 1958 investment classic, *Common Stocks and Uncommon Profits.*[52] Successful execution of such an approach requires an inquisitive mind, a desire to read widely, and a willingness to gather information broadly. Indeed, seeking multiple prongs beyond obvious corporate constituents and into more obscure corners can help.

To this end, our firm employs a large internal market research team to monitor industry and consumer trends for potential structural shifts in momentum. Other relevant sources might include social media (something we have been analyzing since 2010) or trade journals – which can be found even in arcane industries, such as *The Hearing Journal* in the case of audiology. Sometimes such ancillary investigations lead nowhere and rarely do they reveal pivotal data, but they often produce seemingly insignificant points whose relevance crystallizes later in the analytical process when, suddenly, the pieces fall into place.

MISTAKE REDUCTION

Mistakes are inevitable in investing but can be reduced by tools consciously designed to combat their sources as well as refined reflection on past mistakes and current biases. Checklists can help focus rationality and confront the important questions about an investment. Given the complexities, no checklist can capture every nuance or draw attention to every risk. However, using them can facilitate adherence to the principles of quality investing and highlight extraneous top-down factors that may tempt an investment decision, such as stellar short-term growth or an optically low valuation.

A good checklist should enumerate all the desired attributes for an investment and, ideally, the steps required for full due diligence. It should also incorporate lessons learned from previous mistakes and be regularly updated accordingly.

Another useful tool is *inertia analysis*, which compares the hypothetical performance of an unchanged portfolio with actual performance: the comparison reflects how much value trading decisions add (or subtract). The exercise is an acute reminder that doing nothing can be a positive action and weighs every decision against this – another contribution to mistake reduction.

Past mistakes can be dissected to discern causes, context, and patterns. Such autopsies are most effective if they address a wide range of mistakes, realized and unrealized: for example by assessing both purchase and sale decisions that should, or should not, have been made. Forensic self-analysis is not always comfortable, as facing one's errors seldom is, but it helps reduce mistakes.

A final, and vital, practice is attempting to recognize and combat biases. As summarized by Daniel Kahneman in *Thinking, Fast and Slow*, cognitive errors such as confirmation bias, hindsight bias, and outcome bias are rife in the investing world.[53] Many assessments of quality are steeped in them. Tackling such biases is a tough and ceaseless task, among the greatest challenges for any investor. A primary technique for mitigating the influence of biases is to focus as far as possible on the process rather than the outcome: adhering to fundamental investment principles in the face of inevitable market gyrations. However, in a performance-driven world, this is often daunting, evoking Goethe's observation: "To think is easy. To act is hard. But the hardest thing in the world is to act in accordance with your thinking."

EPILOGUE

D EFINITIONS OF CORPORATE GREATNESS AND contests for the most admired companies are often based on factors like breakthrough innovation, recent sales growth, or sheer corporate scale. As quality investors, a major part of how we define greatness is the durability of the economics of the business. Finance theory may be correct that, as a general rule, abnormal outcomes cannot persist – that above-average performance will soon enough become average performance. But quality investing focuses on exceptions to that rule, seeking companies boasting a combination of traits that overcome the forces of mean reversion.

Benefitting from attractive industry structures and unique patterns of competitive advantage, quality companies deliver sustainably higher growth and achieve strong returns on capital over the long term. This combination generates significant value for patient investors. Despite a focus on durability, companies change, and not always for the better. Being alert to spot such transitions early is as important to investment results as identifying quality companies in the first place.

In investing, experience counts. Mistakes and successes help to reveal what works and what fails. If investing were simply about following a rulebook, such practical learning would be unnecessary.

However, a clear, consistent investment philosophy works best if combined with a willingness to adapt and learn from experience. Quality investing is a process of life-long learning rather than a static prescription. We agree with Benjamin Franklin that an "investment in knowledge pays the best interest".

APPENDIX

AKO Capital was founded in October 2005 by Nicolai Tangen and manages approximately $10 billion across long-only and long-short equity funds. It has a long-term investor base that includes many of the world's leading endowments, charitable foundations, institutional investors and sovereign wealth funds. AKO Capital has so far generated approximately $3.4 billion of returns for its investors.

It was nominated for the Eurohedge Best European Equity Fund and Best New European Fund awards in 2006 and for Best European Equity Fund over $500 million in 2009, 2010, 2012 and 2014, winning in 2012.

In the ten years since inception, AKO Capital has grown at a compound annual growth rate more than double that of the market (9.4% per annum versus the MSCI Europe's 3.9%) and outperformed the market in eight out of the nine calendar years 2006-14.[54] For further information please visit: www.akocapital.com

AKO Foundation is a UK-registered charity ultimately funded from the profits of AKO Capital. The Foundation is focused on making grants to projects which improve education or promote the arts and it has, since its inception, been funded by over $50 million.

AKO Capital's royalties from sales of this book will be donated to AKO Foundation.

Endnotes

1.   A2 share class of AKO Fund Limited (the long-short fund) compared with MSCI Europe (Net) in local currency October 1, 2005 to September 30, 2015.

2.   On a ROIC basis, from October 1, 2005 to September 30, 2015 the AKO long book delivered an excess return versus the MSCI Europe of 7.7% per annum (unadjusted) or 8.4% per annum (beta-adjusted). These figures have been calculated using the internal records of AKO Capital.

3.   Robert M. Pirsig, *Zen and the Art of Motorcycle Maintenance: An inquiry into Values* (William Morrow & Company, 1974).

4.   Warren Buffett, Letter to Berkshire Hathaway Shareholders, 1992, reprinted Warren E. Buffett and Lawrence A. Cunningham, *The Essays of Warren Buffett: Lessons of Corporate America* (Carolina Academic Press, 3rd ed. 2013), p. 107.

5.   See Clifford S. Asness, Andrea Frazzini and Lasse H. Pedersen, 'Quality Minus Junk', in CFA Digest, vol. 44, 2013 (www.cfainstitute.org/learning/products/publications/dig/Pages/dig.v44.n1.18.aspx).

In this study, the researchers tested whether the characteristics of quality companies persist. The paper found persistence over the whole ten-year period studied. The study also found that quality companies were more expensive, mostly because of profitability and growth. The safety of companies, on the other hand, showed mixed correlation and was even negative when controlling for other factors. This suggests that while the market tends to spot quality companies, it does not pay a premium for predictability. And the premium pricing does not necessarily mean that the companies are correctly valued.

6.   See, Paul B. Carroll and Chunka Mui, *Billion Dollar Lessons* (Portfolio, 2008). The authors dedicate a whole chapter to a discussion of failed roll-ups,

highlighting that the rapid pace of deal-making in some roll-up strategies make them a conduit for frauds. The authors underline the point that roll-ups where there is no established template for integration and improvement are not generally compelling: "sometimes, roll-ups look like an attempt to stitch together a bunch of rock groups to form an orchestra," p. 61.

7.   See Mark Sirower, *The Synergy Trap* (Simon & Schuster, 2007), p. 14, "many acquisition premiums require performance improvements that are virtually impossible to realise, even for the best of managers in the best of conditions."

A 2004 study by McKinsey (Scott Christofferson, Rob McNish and Diane Sias, 'Where Mergers Go Wrong', McKinsey on Finance, 2004) found that the success rate in delivering post-deal cost synergies was 60%. The majority of companies hit cost targets but cost reductions generally took longer than expected. When it came to revenue synergies, however, the story was very different: 70% of deals failed to hit their top-line synergy targets. Initial goals were often over-inflated due to inadequate due diligence, rosy projections for market growth or underestimating dis-synergies from a merger. In the same report, McKinsey estimates that the average merging company loses 2-5% of its combined customers.

8.   See Peter Lynch, *One Up On Wall Street: How To Use What You Already Know To Make Money In The Market* (Simon & Schuster, 2000).

9.   See Alice Bonaime, Kristine Hankins and Bradford Jordan, 'The Cost of Financial Flexibility: Evidence from Share Repurchases', ssrn.com, 2015.

10.   PWC, *Global Working Capital Review 2013*, p. 26.

11.   Cash return on cash capital invested (CROCCI) is an unlevered, underlying, after tax cash-on-cash return figure. The denominator (gross cash invested) comprises net PPE plus net intangibles plus working capital, accumulated depreciation / amortisation and capitalized leases (but not pension liabilities or assets). The numerator is debt-adjusted cash flow (DACF) – lease-adjusted, after-tax operating cash flow, excluding financing expenses.

12.   CFROI, cash flow return on investment, is Credit Suisse's measure of return on capital; a cash-flow-based proxy for a company's economic return.

13.   Credit Suisse's HOLT team uses the acronym 'eCAP' to describe such stocks. The theory is that such companies enjoy a sustained competitive advantage period (CAP). An eCAP stock is one that has sustained a high CFROI (above 8%) for five years: the eCAP cohort represents about 12% of the European index. By sector, the eCAP universe is significantly overweight Consumer and Healthcare stocks and underweight sectors such as Basic Resources and Utilities.

14.   See Ian Little, 'Higgledy-Piggledy Growth', in *Bulletin of the Oxford University Institute of Economics and Statistics*, 1962.

15.   Bryant Matthews and David A. Holland, 'Prepared for Chance: Forecasting Corporate Growth', February 2015.

16.   Source: Bloomberg data.

17.   For example, over the same 2009-2014 period, the companies in the AKO long book (as at year-end 2014) delivered earnings growth broadly in line with consensus expectations. This did not occur for every company in every year, but in aggregate, these companies broadly delivered against earnings expectations. The outcome was an EPS CAGR of 10% (versus the European market's CAGR of just over 1%).

18.   See Goldman Sachs SUSTAIN publications including, for example, Nick Hartley, 'A renewal of vows', April 2013.

19.   Ulrike Malmendier and Geoffrey Tate, 'Superstar CEOs', in *The Quarterly Journal of Economics* 124:4 (MIT Press, November 2009), pp. 1593-1638.

20.   See Del Jones, 'Some Firms' Fertile Soil Grows Crop of Future CEOs', *USA Today*, 9 January 2008.

21.   Phil Rosenzweig, *The Halo Effect, How Managers Let Themselves Be Deceived* (Pocket Books, 2008).

22.   See John G. Dawes, 'Cigarette Brand Loyalty and Purchase Patterns: An Examination Using US Consumer Panel Data', University of South Australia – Ehrenberg-Bass Institute, 2012.

23.   Ambev's 2014 market share in the Brazilian beer market was c. 68%.

24.   Donald A. Hay and Derek J. Morris, *Industrial Economics and Organization: Theory and Evidence* (Oxford University Press, 1991), p. 200: "the relationship between industrial structure and price setting over times remains very unclear… it is difficult to avoid concluding that, if any such links do exist, they are far from obvious and unlikely to be powerful…Industrial structure may have an important influence on price procedures… but it does not seem to play a central role in the pattern of price changes that develops through time."

25.   The division was sold to EQT Partners in November 2014.

26.   An ostomy is a surgically created opening in the body, usually made to facilitate the discharge of body wastes. One of the global leaders in the market, with 35-40% share, is Danish company Coloplast. The benefits of operating in this niche are reflected in Coloplast's high CFROI (24% in 2014) and elevated operating margins (over 30% on an underlying basis).

27.   Two surveys carried out by AKO's Market Research team support this assertion. In August 2013, we conducted a consumer survey with 1000 affluent consumers aged 21-74 in the United States (boasting annual household income exceeding $200,000). If consumer confidence deteriorated, more than half of respondents (55%) indicated that they were "not at all likely" or "not very likely" to reduce spending on their physical appearance (hair, skin, make-up). The only category in which they were less likely to reduce spending (among 15) was education. In August 2015, we also conducted interviews amongst 711 'mass affluent' consumers in China with a monthly household income of at least RMB 16,000. If consumer confidence deteriorated, our Chinese respondents indicated that they would, on balance, reduce spend on physical appearance.

However, once again this category ranked as the second most resilient category, after education.

28. See P. Peeters, J. Middel and A. Hoolhorst, 'Fuel efficiency of commercial aircraft. An overview of historical and future trend', 2005 (airneth.nl).

29. The company employs over 11,000 service professionals across 160 locations in 70 different countries.

30. See interview by Louella-Mae Eleftheriou-Smith, 'Ryanair's Michael O'Leary: Short of committing murder, bad publicity sells more seats', 1 August 2013 (marketingmagazine.co.uk).

31. McKinsey & Company, 'The Five Attributes of Enduring Family Businesses', 2010.

32. McKinsey & Company, 'Perspectives on Founder- and Family-Owned Businesses', 2014; and 'Family Firms: Business in the blood', in *The Economist*, November 2014.

33. Cristina Cruz Serrano and Laura Nuñez Letamendia, 'Value Creation in Listed European family firms (2001-2010)', *Academy Management Journal* (2015).

34. 'The unsung masters of the oil industry', *The Economist*, June 2012.

35. Safilo relisted in December 2005 at over €60/ share, since which point its share price has declined over 80% in absolute terms.

36. Back-testing Credit Suisse's HOLT data, we found that a strategy of owning eCAP stocks (eCAPs refer to stocks which have sustained superior CFROI over five or more years) would have delivered outperformance of the Global market in 15 out of the last 20 years. This is broadly consistent with the findings of the Goldman Sachs SUSTAIN team, which see an even more consistent long-term pattern of outperformance by first quartile CROCCI companies on a sector relative basis.

37. AKO conducted a study of profit-warnings across 644 companies from Q1'04 through Q2'13 (and excluding the crisis years of 2007 and 2008) and found the following:

- The worse the profit-warning, the worse the subsequent performance (i.e. performance excluding the initial share price drop accompanying the profit warning) versus the index. This is particularly true for companies whose reported numbers caused an initial share price decline of at least 10%.

- The more frequently a company profit-warns, the worse it performs after its latest profit-warning. This means, for example, that the stock of a company that has its second 10% profit-warning within a year will perform worse than the stock of a company issuing its first profit-warning.

- Companies with lower CFROI tend to profit-warn more frequently and perform worse after profit-warnings than companies with higher CFROI. The difference in performance after a profit warning is significant: all else equal, a high CFROI (CFROI higher than 15%) will outperform a low CFROI (lower than 5%) by just over 10% on average after a profit warning.

- About one-third of companies that issue large profit-warnings, defined as initial share price drops of 10% or more, have more than one large profit-warning within a year. The subsequent profit-warnings are, on average, larger.

- Companies with recent CEO changes tend to profit-warn a bit more frequently than companies with no CEO changes.

- Companies that profit-warn after CEO changes tend to outperform the index.

38. Market Force Information survey of 6,800 people, published in *The Grocer* magazine, June 2015.

39. Ilia Dichev, John Graham, Campbell Harvey and Shivaram Rajgopal, 'Earnings Quality: Evidence From the Field' (working paper), 2012.

40. Premature revenue recognition: Companies typically accelerate (pull forward) revenue by offering rebates and/or offering more liberal credit terms – which expire at the end of a period – to entice customers to purchase more than they need in the period. While this practice can lead to higher revenue in the period, such revenues tend to reduce in future periods. A material increase in receivables levels might indicate such practices. Revenue recognition chicanery is prevalent among companies adopting the so-called percentage-of-completion method, which grants managers vast discretion over the timing, amount and classification of revenue. Red flags appear in the relative levels of revenue recognized, amounts billed to customers, and advance billings (deferred revenue).

41. Inflated gross margins: The most common technique to inflate gross margin is overproduction. When a company overproduces, its fixed costs are distributed over more units, thereby boosting gross margins. An increase in inventory levels, relative both to cost of goods sold and next period revenue, could indicate overproduction and overstated gross margins. In addition, if a company's inventory levels are too high, its future gross margins may come under pressure from slower production, discounting and/or obsolescence charges.

42. Improperly capitalized expenses: By improperly capitalizing expenses, a company records operating expense as an asset and inflates operating profits. Operating expenses most prone to aggressive or improper capitalization are research and development, software development, customer acquisition, labor and overhead for long-term projects. The most typical signs of improperly capitalized expenses are unexplained spikes in capitalized expense versus total expenses and capitalized expenses in a period.

43. Depleting reserves: Depleting reserves is a common earnings management technique. In good times, a company builds reserves such as allowances for bad debts; in bad times, it boosts earnings by reversing or not replenishing them. Any decline in reserves relative to the related account – such as accounts receivable in the case of allowance for bad debt – represents an unsustainable boost to earnings. In the United States, such practices are often referred to as 'cookie jar reserves'.

44. Manipulated cash flows: Among common ways to manipulate cash flows are: sales/factoring of receivables, extending payables, and improperly capitalizing expenditures. By selling/factoring receivables, a company converts receivables into cash before the cash is due from customers, which results in inflated cash generation in the period of sale. This is done by a company transferring ownership of receivables to an investor (typically a bank) in exchange for cash less fees. In addition to providing unsustainable boosts to cash flows from operations, this practice can also mask a 'pulling-forward' of revenue. Of course, factoring is a standard practice in many industries, so discerning intent can be both important and difficult.

By extending payables a company simply defers payment of its obligations to a later period, thereby unsustainably boosting operating cash flows in a current period. Although this cash flow management technique is transparent, companies still use it to some extent to boost or smooth operating cash flows. By improperly capitalizing expenses, a company records operating expense as an asset, which, in addition to inflating operating profits, also inflates operating cash flows.

45. The basic idea of business valuation is simple, but applying it is often fiendishly difficult. From a theoretical perspective, the value of a financial asset is equal to its future cash flows discounted back to today at an appropriate rate. In practice, this mathematical ideal quickly hits stumbling blocks, starting with the notorious difficulty of forecasting cash flows. The best way to get the practice to meet the ideal is to work with companies whose cash flows are most predictable – and to avoid the rest.

Finance theory and stock market practice stipulate that all companies can be valued – even those with erratic cash flow histories – by selecting the appropriate discount rate. Among popular tools for discount rate selection is beta, derived from a company's relative historical stock price volatility. Despite its popularity, beta is widely criticized, especially because it can be difficult to defend the assertion that stock price volatility is a good proxy for business risk that determines future cash flows. Certainly the owners of private businesses do not evaluate business risk using such tools.

In any event, discount rates do not probe the greatest risk investors face, which is the permanent loss of capital. If the value of an investment irredeemably erodes, the relevant cause is always the firm's business analysis: there was something about the company's future prospects that the investor failed to account for. With this starting point, it is far more sensible to avoid companies lacking predicable cash flows than trying to forecast an erratic pattern and adjust for risk using arbitrary tools such as beta.

46. See Goldman Sachs SUSTAIN publications including, for example, Nick Hartley, 'A renewal of vows', April 2013.

47. See Chuck Joyce and Kimball Mayer, 'Profits for the Long Run: Affirming the Case for Quality', GMO 2012. This study examined 1,000 large US companies

from 1965-2012 based on financial variables commonly associated with quality. The factors used to indicate quality were low leverage, high profitability, low profit volatility and low beta. The study compared performance of the companies in the highest quartile and compared it to benchmark returns. The factors all delivered annual outperformance versus benchmark over the period. The results ranged from 0.8% for low leverage to 0.4% for high profitability and low profit volatility. Low beta, which by its own definition should yield below-market returns, delivered annualized outperformance of 0.5%.

48. Another source of market bias and pricing error is the skewed incentive to accumulate assets. Global equity markets remain dominated by long-only institutional investors that make the vast majority of their money from assets under management. Inflows into asset managers are determined by historical performance. But inflows are far greater when stock market averages rise than when they fall. To outperform in rising (bull) markets, therefore, becomes more valuable than outperforming in bear markets, when equity markets decline. This skews demand towards stocks with the potential to rise in price more than average in bull markets (high beta stocks) and away from stocks that are predictable and shine more consistently in bull and bear markets alike (low beta stocks).

An institutional bias towards high-beta stocks may contribute yet another source of quality underpricing. Quality companies, because of their relative predictability growth and stable earnings, often have lower betas. A study comparing such categories concluded that investors are willing to overpay for high-beta stocks compared to low-beta stocks. See Frazzini and Pedersen, 'Betting Against Beta', 9 October 2011. This was attributed to the fact that most institutional investors are restricted from using leverage. Consequently, they must overweight high-beta stocks to generate higher returns than their benchmark. This stokes artificially strong demand for high-beta stocks relative to low-beta stocks.

49. Source: Datastream. Average US mutual fund holding periods have been consistently under one year for the past five years.

50. Source: Goldman Sachs SUSTAIN: 'Returns and Alpha' (presentation), 6 September 2011.

51. "There is a strong presumption in economics that, in a competitive environment, profitability is mean reverting." Eugene F. Fama and Kenneth R. French, 'Forecasting Profitability and Earnings', 2000, p. 161.

52. Philip Fisher, *Common Stocks and Uncommon Profits* (Harper Bros, 1958).

53. Daniel Kahneman, *Thinking, Fast and Slow* (Farrar, Straus and Giroux, 2011).

54. A2 share class of AKO Fund Limited (the long-short fund) compared with MSCI Europe (Net) in local currency October 1, 2005 to September 30, 2015.

INDEX

reduction of 175–7
of retention 163–70
when buying 158–62
Moët & Chandon 41, 94
Molin, Johan 15
Mondelēz 40
monopolies 40, 52, 56, 84–5, 87, 166
mini-monopolies 35–6, 84, 101
partial 37, 40
Monsanto 54, 87
Moody's Investors Service 73
Morrisons 165
MSN Chat 57
Munger, Charlie 151
Munters 33
MySpace 57

Nestlé 40, 47, 104, 111
network benefits 66
network density 66
network effects 56–7
new entrants 141–2
newness, danger of 92
next-Monday optimism 159–60
niche sector 43
Nike 26, 93–4, 101, 103–4
Nintendo 92
Nivea 45
Nobel Biocare 145–7
Nokia 5, 137–8
Novartis 54
Novo Nordisk 99–100, 171
Noyce, Robert 135

Oakley 14, 93, 104–5
O'Leary, Michael 33, 82
oligopolies 38–9, 77
online presence 103–5
OPEC countries 131
OPSM 105
optimism 159–60
Otis Elevators 68
overconfidence 160–1

Pan Am 89

partial monopolies 37, 40
patent protection 52
Pearle Vision 105
Pedersen, Harald 99
Pepsi 21, 38
Pierre Cardin 94
Pizza Hut 111
PlayStation 92
Polaroid 54
Polo Ralph Lauren 104, 141
Prada 104
Pratt & Whitney 110
predictability 160–1
premium brands 26, 93–4
premiumization 97
price deflation 87–8
pricing 26–7, 41
power 84–8
premium 89–90
for value 87
Primark 78
Procter & Gamble 46
product mix 26–7
product upfront 62–3
profit margins 21–2

qualitative judgments 155–6

Ramo, Si 121
rationality 39–40
mechanisms 40–1
Ray-Ban 89, 104–5
Reckitt Benckiser 98
recurring revenue
economic effects 66–8
license model 63
product upfront 62–3
service model 64–5
subscriptions 65–6
research and development (R&D) 9,
12–13, 22, 39, 46, 53, 55, 72, 94–6,
106, 115, 120, 168–9
R&D-led innovation 98–100
retail consumers 50
return on equity 19–21